A GUIDE TO TRACING YOUR KERRY ANCESTORS

A guide to tracing your Kerry ancestors

by Michael H. O'Connor

FLYLEAF PRESS

2nd Edition 1994

First Published 1990 by
Flyleaf Press,

4 Spencer Villas,
Glenageary,
Co. Dublin,
Ireland,

© 1990 Flyleaf Press

British Library Cataloguing in Publication Data
O'Connor, Michael H., 1964-
A guide to tracing your Kerry ancestors
1. Ireland. Genealogy. Research
I.Title
929.107209415

ISBN 0-9508466-51

Cover design by Cathy Henderson

Printed by Colour Books, Dublin

Table of Contents

Acknowledgements

While writing this book I have been assisted by many people. My wife Carolyn and son Daniel have been most patient and helpful over the last two years. I couldn't have done this without their support. Carolyn also edited the initial versions of the book a number of times and did some of the typing. Dr. James Ryan has brought his expertise in the field of Irish genealogy to bear on the editing of this book, which is much better for his efforts. Pádraig Concubhair of Lenamore, County Kerry gave his support, encouragement and ideas. Michael Costelloe and the staff at the County Kerry Library in Tralee have been extremely helpful. The staff at the many public institutions in Australia, Ireland, the United States and England which hold County Kerry records always gave assistance. Judy Thomson, my sister-in-law, and my sister Elizabeth O'Connor gave valuable assistance with the collecting of material. Dr Kate Hammond and Dr Louise Prentice provided assistance with the collection of some headstone transcripts.

The detailed comments of Richard M. Doherty of Troy, Missouri, USA enhanced the quality of the second edition.

Abbreviations

BL	British Library
b.	born/birth.
Co.	County.
CDB	Congested Districts Board.
CUL	Cambridge University Library, England.
d.	died/death.
DNS	Did Not Survive.
DKPRI	(Reports of the) Deputy Keeper of Public Records of Ireland.
GRO	General Registrar's Office
IGI	International Genealogical Index.
ILC	Irish Land Commission
IMC	Irish Manuscripts Commission.
JAPMD	Journal of the Association for the Preservation of the Memorials of the Dead in Ireland.
JKAHS	Journal of the County Kerry Archaeological and Historical Society.
J.Kilk. AHS	Journal of the Kilkenny Archaeological and Historical Society.
JSK	County Kerry Past and Present: A Guide to the Local and Family History of the County, by Jeremiah S. King, Dublin, 1931.
KCL	Kerry County Library.
KEP	Kerry Evening Post (see p. 63).
KPS	Kildare Place Society (see p. 73).
LDS	Church of Jesus-Christ of Latter-Day Saints.
m.	married.
MAH	Mary Agnes Hickson's book Selections of Old Kerry Records.
MFCI	Microfilm of Church of Ireland Records.
NAI	National Archives of Ireland. (Formerly the PRO.)
NLI	National Library of Ireland.
OCM	O'Kiefe, Coshe Mang, Slieve Lougher and Upper Blackwater in Ireland, vols. 1 to 15, Dr A.E. Casey, Birmingham (USA).
Pub.	Published.
PRO	Public Record Office, Dublin, Ireland — see NAI
PROK	Public Record Office, Kew, London, England.
PRONI	Public Record Office of Northern Ireland.
RCBL	Representative Church Body Library.
RGO	Registrar-Generals Office, Dublin.
RIA	Royal Irish Academy.
RSAI	Royal Society of Antiquarians in Ireland.

Chapter 1   Introduction

The Irish word for Kerry is Ciarrai or Ciarraige, the name of a tribe of Celts who were once prominent in the south-west of Ireland. The original Celtic settlers in County Kerry arrived in two waves; the Erainn about 500 B.C. and the Eoganacht about 50 B.C. Other Celtic groups made their way to Co. Kerry from other parts of Ireland. These tribes are the original ancestors of many of the Kerry people of today. There have been other immigrants since that time, the Danes, the Normans, the English, Huguenot French and Palatine Germans. All of these cultures have contributed to the unique character of the Kerryman of the twentieth century.

The nineteenth-century was a period of great change in Co. Kerry (and indeed in all of Ireland). Many people left Co. Kerry, to live elsewhere in Ireland, or for the chance of a new life in countries such as Australia, New Zealand, U.S.A., Canada and England. For those that remain in Kerry, and for those who are currently 'in exile', this book represents a means to establish or re-establish their Co. Kerry origins.

The chapters of this guide describe the major historical records useful to a researcher of Co. Kerry ancestry. Two unfortunate fires (1711,1922) have eliminated many useful records. The positive outcome of these destructive events has been that Irish archivists have acquired valuable material which they might not otherwise have considered retaining. The National Archives in Dublin holds more material now than it did before the 1922 fire!

Many researchers will be tracing ancestors with rural Catholic origins. From the 1650's until the late 1800's, this group's right to own land and property gradually reduced and then increased again. As a result fewer written records were made in regard to them, particularly during the 18th century. Most Church registers commence in the early part of the nineteenth century. Registrations of births, deaths and marriages by the state commence in 1864 (except Church of Ireland marriages). However much progress may be made despite these difficulties, and for some Catholic and non-Catholic families, detailed family histories are available.

The researcher should consider that every source may have value. This guide is valuable because it discusses the content and value of the many scattered sources in a single comprehensive volume. The surviving records for Co. Kerry are listed in separate chapters under the headings:

3.   Administrative Divisions
4.   Censuses and Census Substitutes
5.   Church Records
6.   Civil Registration of Births, Deaths and Marriages
7.   Commercial and Social Directories
8.   Wills and Administrations
9.   Memorial Inscriptions
10. Land Tenure and Ownerships
11. Newspapers
12. National and Local Government Records
13. Military Records
14. Education Records
15. Family Histories
16. General Kerry References
17. Useful Addresses

Chapter 2   How to use this Book

Genealogy, the study of the relationships between people in places in time, relies on the records of the ancestor's existence (birth, land ownership, death etc) for its basic information, and local history for its backdrop and its historical relevance. The latter local history sources may be a major means of locating the former primary records. Thus I have not been strict in limiting the contents of this book to sources that only state who was born, married or died and where and when. The sources in this book are both primary sources; church registers, newspapers etc; and secondary sources such as local histories and journal articles.

Successful Co. Kerry Family Research

Each family history researcher has their own approach to doing research. Most successful research has three common elements, which should be applied to Co. Kerry ancestral research.

a) Set a Goal: Decide which branch of the family you wish to trace and in which direction. Although you may start your research only knowing a single Co. Kerry ancestor, when you find the ancestor's parents you have two branches to trace and so forth. Trying to trace all branches is a daunting task hence the requirement for a research goal.

b) Work from the known to the unknown: Use the details of those ancestors you have the most amount of information about to locate other ancestors. An inexperienced researcher might find mention (in a family tree or history book) of a family of the same name as their ancestor and try to prove that the documented family is related. The proper approach is to attempt to locate ancestors using the information you already know from prior research.

c) Work from the more recent to the most distant: Generally more recent records of the events of a persons life are likely to have survived. That is, use the record of death or burial to indicate the probable year of marriage, which in turn may indicate the year of birth.

Records in Your Home Country

The initial searching for County Kerry ancestors must usually be done wherever the family live now, through genealogy societies and the genealogical resources of the Church of Latter-Day Saints, and larger public and private libraries. Useful sources in these countries include many of the same record categories listed in this book; censuses, church records and civil registration.

The Irish Records

The historical records of Co. Kerry are generally linked to some form of administrative division (see Chapter 3). A thorough knowledge of these divisions is essential for successful research and for understanding the organisation of the records mentioned in the other chapters of this book. The chapters are ordered so that the more useful and easily accessible record categories are presented at the front. Each search for ancestry is different, therefore the researcher must determine which records to search, and in which order. Copies of many Irish records exist outside of Ireland. Where known they are listed in this book because they may save some researchers a trip to Ireland (a thoroughly enjoyable place to do research nonetheless). Chapter 17 lists the major relevant record repositories in Ireland, UK, Australia and the USA which hold copies of Irish records and other chapters of the book note the items which are to be found in these countries.

Chapter 3   Administrative divisions

During the last two thousand years Co. Kerry has been divided into a number of different areas for the purpose of civil and ecclesiastical (church) administration. The records made by these administrations are listed throughout this book. To understand the locations or addresses mentioned in historical records a thorough knowledge of the various divisions is essential.

Civil Divisions

The civil divisions of Ireland relevant to Co. Kerry are described in this section, starting with the largest, the province, and finishing with the smallest, the townland.

Province: Co. Kerry is in Munster province. The provinces roughly correspond to four ancient Irish kingdoms. The other counties in Munster are Limerick, Cork, Waterford, Tipperary and Clare.

County: The county is the major administrative division of land and is an autonomous unit for many administrative purposes. Co. Kerry is adjacent to two other counties, namely Limerick in the North and Cork in the South. Co. Clare is just across the Shannon River.

Barony: Baronies correspond to ancient tribal or clan regions in many cases. The barony has little administrative significance but occurs in older records. Co. Kerry has nine baronies (see map on p. 17), Iraghticonnor, Clanmaurice, Corkaguiny, Trughanacmy, Magunihy, Iveragh, Dunkerron North, Dunkerron South and Glanarought.

Poor Law Union: The Poor Law Relief Act of 1838 was instituted to alleviate the severe distress of the poor in Ireland. The whole country was divided into Poor Law Unions, for the purpose of administering relief to the poor. Each Union, centered on a single town, was further divided into Electoral divisions, the names of which are listed in the General Alphabetical Index of Ireland (see the end of this section for details). The chapter on Local Government (chap. 12) lists the records of the Unions. Civil registration records (p.41) and the Continuing Valuation records use the Poor Law Union as a means of organisation.

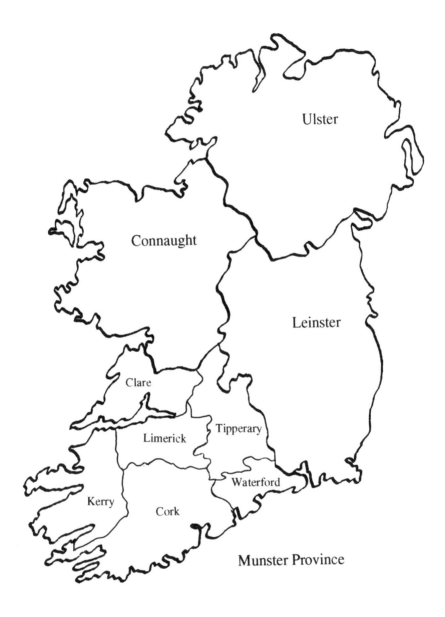

Map of Ireland showing boundaries of Kerry and the other Munster Counties

Civil Parish: The Civil Parish (see map on p. 17) is the key to finding your Irish ancestors as most record categories embrace this geographical division. An interesting feature of the civil parish is that several unconnected areas of land many kilometres apart may be part of the same civil parish. Civil parishes may cross county boundaries, for instance, Kilcaskan and Nohovaldaly are partly in Co. Cork. There are 87 civil parishes in Co. Kerry.

Townland: This is the smallest administrative unit of land and varies in size from 10 to thousands of acres. It is the basic address used by rural Irish people. Each civil parish is comprised of a number of townlands. A town or village might comprise parts of a number of different townlands.

The standard reference work "General Alphabetical Index to Townlands and Towns, Parishes and Baronies of Ireland" (first published by Thom's Dublin 1851, reprinted 1984 by Genealogical Publishing Co., Baltimore, USA). This is based on the places listed in the 1851 census, is useful for locating and verifying placenames.

Ecclesiastical Divisions

Ecclesiastically Co. Kerry is part of the historical Diocese of Ardfert and Aghadoe for both the Church of Ireland and the Catholic Church. Today the Catholic diocese is called Kerry. The Church of Ireland Diocese is important as certain records were historically administered by the Church of Ireland as the established church, eg Wills and Administrations (p. 45). The types of Ecclesiastical Divisions are:

Church of Ireland Parish: In most cases the Church of Ireland parish is consistent with the Civil Parish and has the same name.

Catholic Parish: There are 45 Catholic parishes in Co. Kerry. Unlike Church of Ireland parishes, most do not conform to the boundaries of the civil parish, and will often not have the same name as the civil parishes they comprise. A single Catholic parish may include more than one civil parish, or one civil parish may cover several different Catholic parishes. (see Church Records on p. 28).

Church of Ireland Diocese: The Diocese Ardfert and Aghadoe is an amalgamation of 2 ancient dioceses of which Aghadoe administered the south of Co. Kerry. Historical records organised by diocese always include the two dioceses together. The diocese includes most of Co. Kerry except for the parish of Kilcaskan in Glanarought barony, which is in the Diocese of Ross.

Catholic Diocese: The Catholic Diocese of Kerry includes almost the whole of County Kerry except for a single townland in the parish of Tarbert (Kilmurrily) and also parts of County Cork.

Civil Parish List

The map on the opposite page shows the civil parishes and baronies of Co. Kerry. The civil parishes can be located using the numbering scheme listed below:

1	Kilconly	30	Killiney	59	Currans
2	Aghavallen	31	Kilgobban	60	Killeentierna
3	Kilnaughten	32	Dunurlin	61	Dysert
4	Killehenny	33	Marhin	62	Kilcolman
5	Lisselton	34	Kilmalkedar	63	Killorglin
6	Galey	35	Dingle	64	Valentia
7	Murher	36	Garfinny	65	Caher
8	Ballyconry	37	Kinard	66	Killinane
9	Listowel	38	Minard	67	Glanbeigh
10	Knockanure	39	Ballynacourty	68	Killemlagh
11	Killury	40	Ballinvoher	69	Prior
12	Rattoo	41	Dunquin	70	Dromod
13	Dysert	42	Ventry	71	Knockane
14	Finuge	43	Kildrum	72	Molahiffe
15	Duagh	44	Fenit	73	Kilnanare
16	Ballyheigue	45	Ballynahaglish	74	Kilbonane
17	Killahan	46	Clogherbrien	75	Aglish
18	Kiltomy	47	Tralee	76	Kilcredane
19	Kilcaragh	48	Ratass	77	Kilcummin
20	Kilfeighny	49	Ballymacelligott	78	Nohovaldaly
21	Kilshenane	50	O'Brennan	79	Aghadoe
22	Kilmoyly	51	Castleisland	80	Killarney
23	O'Dorney	52	Brosna	81	Killaha
24	Kilflyn	53	Annagh	82	Kilcrohane
25	Ardfert	54	Ballyseedy	83	Templenoe
26	Kilquane	55	Nohoval	84	Kenmare
27	Cloghane	56	Ballincuslane	85	Kilgarvan
28	Ballyduff	57	Kilgarrylander	86	Tuosist
29	Stradbally	58	Kiltallagh	87	Kilcaskan

Civil Parish/Barony Map

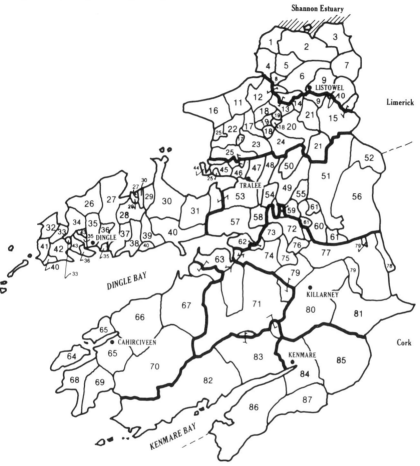

⌐ = CIVIL PARISHES ADJOINING ACROSS
BARONY BOUNDARIES.

BARONIES

1. IRAGHTICONNOR
2. CLANMAURICE
3. CORKAGUINY
4. TRUGHANACMY
5. IVERAGH
6. DUNKERRON. N.
7. MAGUNIHY
8. DUNKERRON S.
9. GLANAROUGHT

Gazetteers

A gazetteer is a dictionary or index of geographical names, useful for locating and validating Co. Kerry placenames encountered during research. The major reference for this task, General Alphabetical Index to Townlands etc. is described on p. 15. The following references also contain descriptions of Co. Kerry placenames.

Lewis, S., *A Topographical Dictionary of Ireland*, Dublin, 1837. Reprinted in 1984. Civil parishes as well as many towns and villages are described.

King, J.S., *County Kerry Past and Present: Handbook to Local and Family History*, Hodges, Figgis and Co., Dublin, 1931. Each townland, parish and barony in Co. Kerry is discussed in this volume. A list of *Townlands in Kerry* is available in the above and is reprinted in OCM vol. 8.

Barony, Parish and Townland Consolidated Index, Co. Kerry, 1641-1851 from all major sources of this period is printed in OCM vol. 8.

Maps

Co. Kerry has been mapped in varying degrees of detail and accuracy since the 16th century. An important set of maps for family history researchers are the Ordnance Survey maps which were surveyed from 1824. These were used as a basis for conducting the Griffith's Valuation (in Co. Kerry in 1851 and 1852 — see p. 22). Photocopies of the Valuation maps are available from the Valuation Office (see p. 87). In 1913 the Ordnance Survey Office published a set of Townland Index maps which show the outlines of the townlands, parishes, location of churches, towns and schools.

For the 18th century, a collection of road maps is available in G. Taylor and A. Skinner's, "Maps of the Roads of Ireland 1779-1783." The Kerry maps are reprinted in OCM vol. 8. under the title "Towns and Roads In Cork and Kerry 1779-1783". This series of maps shows the sites of churches, roads, castles, and houses of principal gentry. The Down Survey, started in late 1654 by Sir William Petty, was a map based record of land ownership in Ireland. Unfortunately the original parish maps for Co. Kerry, showing details of ownership, did not survive, except for one parish. A certified copy of the Down Survey map for the civil parish of Killeheny, barony of Iraghticonnor is held in the ILC collection, EC 3554, Box 3777 (see the Keane catalog at the NLI for further details). For the other Co. Kerry parishes all that remain are the barony maps, which show the names of townlands but nothing further. This collection, known as Hibernia Regnum is available at the NLI. Other maps of Co. Kerry are noted in the chapter on Land Tenure and Ownership (see p.58).

the high street immediately opposite the Kenmare Arms.

Kerry possesses pre-eminently one distinction for which it has long been famous – the ardour with which its natives acquire and communicate knowledge. It is by no means rare to find among the humblest of the peasantry who have no prospects but that of existing by daily labour, men who can converse fluently in Latin, and have a good knowledge of Greek. However, a more general spread of information and the increased facilities for acquiring it have deprived Kerry of the honour of being exclusively the seat of peasant learning in Ireland. But its inhabitants are still remarkable for the study of dead languages, acquaintance with which has been formed by the greater proportion of them literally under a hedge.

The genuine 'hedge schools' of Kerry are rapidly disappearing, and necessarily with them the old school masters who were in some respects a meritorious, and in others, a pernicious class, for whenever there was disaffection the village school master was either the originator or the sustainer of it. He was also generally the secretary of illegal associations, the writer of threatening notices and too frequently the planner and leader in terrible outrages. The national system of education has destroyed their power by substituting in their places men who are, at all events, responsible to employers interested in their good characters and good conduct. The ancient Domines however, had their merits: they kept alive the shrivelled seed of knowledge from utterly perishing.

During our recent visit we saw but two or three hedge schools: some twenty years ago we should have encountered at least one in every parish. They received their peculiar designation from the fact that, in fine weather, the school room was always removed out-of-doors, with the Domine usually seated beside his threshold and the young urchins, his pupils, scattered about him.

In addition to the pupils who paid to the teacher as much as they could afford and in the coin most at their command, there were generally some in such establishments who paid nothing, and were not expected to pay anything. They were termed 'poor scholars'

Sample page from "Hall's Ireland: Mr and Mrs Hall's Tour of 1840."
Hall, Virtue & Co., London, 1841

Narrative Descriptions

During the 18th and the nineteenth century many gentry engaged in what was known as a tour. That is, they went on a trip around Ireland and then published a description of what they saw and sometimes who they met on their travels. They are useful as narrative descriptions of the conditions of the period in which they were written. Many were published and some journal articles have been written about these books. The following is a list of some of the better known works relating to Co. Kerry:

Barrow, John, *A Tour round Ireland: through the sea coast counties in the autumn of 1835*, London, 1836.

Froude, J.A., *A Fortnight in Kerry* in Short Studies on Great Subjects, series 2, pp.179-213 and pp.353-392, London, 1871.

Inglis, H.D., *Ireland in 1834. A journey through Ireland during the Spring and Summer and Autumn of 1834 . . .*, 2 vols, London, 1834.

Smith, Charles, *The Ancient and Present State of the County of Kerry*, Dublin, 1756.

Twiss, R., *A Tour in Ireland in 1775*, London, 1776.

Young, A., *A Tour in Ireland 1776 - 1779*, 2 vols, London, 1780.

Further Reading

The following journal articles discuss further sources for place names and will broaden the reader's knowledge of this topic.

William Molyneaux's geographical collections for Kerry by William O'Sullivan in JKAHS, no. 4 (1971).

Some travellers in Kerry by Sean O'Luing, JKAHS, no. 1 (1968).

Samuel Molyneaux's tour of Kerry, 1709 by Theodore Hoppen and Pádraig de Brún in JKAHS, no. 3 (1970).

Sir Richard Cox's description of Kerry, 1687 by Pádraig de Brún in JKAHS, no. 5 (1972).

Lord Orrery's travels in Kerry, 1735 by The Knight of Glin in JKAHS, no. 5, (1972).

Lewis Dillwyn's Visit to Kerry, 1809 by Gerard J. Lyne in JKAHS, no. 15-16 (1982-83).

A Tour of John Windele's in South Kerry, 1848 by Michael Herity in JKAHS, no. 3 (1970).

Chapter 4   Censuses & Census Substitutes

Official government censuses have been carried out in Ireland at 10-year intervals from 1821 until very recent times, when the census interval changed. However most of the 19th century returns were destroyed in the Public Record Office (PRO) fire in 1922 and few returns survive for Co. Kerry. Various substitutes exist and, while they are not as good as official Government census records, they do have value to the family history researcher. The surviving records are listed below from most recent to most distant in time.

1911

The 1911 census survives for the whole of Co. Kerry. The Census Household Returns contain a complete list of the persons in each household plus ages, religion, ability to read/write, languages spoken, occupation, relationship to head of the household and region of birth (Country or County). The original householder returns are stored at the National Archives of Ireland (NAI) and microfilm copies may be viewed through the LDS.

1908-1922

The Old Age Pension was introduced in Ireland in 1908. To be eligible a pensioner had to prove their age and place of birth. Since birth registration did not begin until 1864 proof was, in many ways, obtained by making certified copies of an 1821-1851 Census return in which the applicant was listed. Surviving Pension application forms from the period 1908-1922 are kept at the NAI. Relatively few of these have survived for Co. Kerry. Obviously they can only exist if a member of your family had remained in Ireland until after 1908. The KEP of August 18, 1909 discusses the eligibility rules for the Old Age Pensions in Ireland.

Be warned that some of the pension forms were for unsuccessful searches of the census records and only contain details of the applicant. A sample from the index shows the type of material available. The names in parentheses are the married names of female applicants.

Civil Parish	Townland	Surname	Year
Aghavallin	Aghanagran	O'Connor (Enright)	1851
	Lenamore	Mahony (Fennel)	1851
Kilnaughtin	Shanaway	O'Connor	1851
Kilconly	Kilconly	Connor	1851
Murher	Kilbaha	Hudson (O'Connor)	1851

1901

The 1901 Census covers the whole of Co. Kerry. The householder returns contain the same information as the 1911 census. The original householder returns are stored at the NAI and microfilm copies may be viewed through the LDS. *County Kerry, Past and Present* by J.S. King's book contains what is almost certainly an index to the 1901 census for Co. Kerry. The index is sorted by surname within the body of the book.

1851-52

Griffith's Valuation, or the Primary Valuation of Tenements was surveyed in Co. Kerry during 1852 except for the civil parish of Dunquin, which was surveyed in 1851. For each townland in each civil parish the name of the landowner/leaseholder is given, along with the lessor, a description of the property, the area of land, and the annual monetary valuation. The valuation was used to levy land taxes or "rates". The non-survival of official censuses for the nineteenth century makes the Valuation very important as a census substitute.

The surnames in the Tithe Applotment Survey (see 1825-1837) and Griffiths Valuation Survey have been indexed by the NLI. The index contains a barony-by-barony index of surnames. Having located the baronies in which the required surname is recorded, proceed to the civil parish indexes which are arranged by civil parish within barony. Having located the parish(es) proceed to the actual valuation to locate the name you seek.

The printed Valuation is a summary of three sets of note books now deposited at the NAI, Dublin; House, Tenure and Field Books. The Tenure books in particular note farm content, tenure details and observations. These books may give the information needed to find a Deed of Lease at the Registry of Deeds.

The original valuation was taken in Co. Kerry in 1851/52 and has been used as a basis for land valuation until recent times. Continuing Valuation Lists from 1855 to 1968 are stored at the Valuation Office in Dublin and the LDS has microfilmed these records up to 1900 for Co. Kerry. They have value for tracing the leaseholder/landowners of land during the 1851 to 1900 period. These

newspapers.

Guards, civic, police constables, re-placed the R.I.C.; the ancient Irish system of having a brugaid for each baile, and a parish council of brug-aids with the parish priest as chair-man, all unpaid, should be the unit of government in Erin now; the English system of centralised gov-ernment from Dublin, by paid police, soldiers, and civil servants, should be discontinued, and taxation for the employment of paid officials could be abolished then.

Guare; Mce. of Trieneragh, Pat of Foildarrig, John of Knockavallig.

Guerin, O'Gearain; 27 families in Kerry, viz.: Jerh. of Cloghereen, John of Gortahoonig, Anne of Flem-ing's lane, Mary and Con and John and Mary of High street, Pat of Gortaree, Mary of Rockfield, Con and John of Tullig, John of Knock-aninane, Rd. of Garryantanavally, Dan and Pat of Dooncaha, Con of Knockundervaul, Pat of Listowel, Jas. of Ballygrennan, Mary of High street, Pat of Mill road, Jerh. of Stealroe, Pat of Killoughane, Denis of Kilnabrack, Pat of Moulnahone, John of Cooleanig, John of Main street, Pat of Garraneareagh.

Guhard, baile in Lisselton; cave here.

Guihan, O'Gaoitin, Guiheen, Guihean; Pat of Strand road, Ml. of Ballintlea, John of Ballineanig, John and Pat and Ml. and Pat and Ml. of Great Blasket island, Ml. of Ballinahow, Tom of Claddanure, Ml. of Kenmare, Julia of Rossmore island, and Ml. of Lehud.

Guinaw, O'Guinide; Dan of Cloona-fineela.

Guiney, O'Guinide, Geany, Guinea; David and Con and Eneas and Ellen of Knockavinna, Denis of Knockeen-creen, Ben and Tim and Mary of Glountaunluskeha, John and Ml. of Knockadarrive, Roger of Lackbro-der, Johanna of Knocknagoshel, Aneas of Brosna, Jas. of Cleeny, Mary of Tooreenascarthy, Pat of Knocknaseed, Pat of Buddaghauns, Wm. and Johanna of Moyvane, Tom of Tieraclea, Pat of Coolaclarig. See Corcaguiney, Corco Duibne, Duben's race.

Guinnell, Delia of Princes quay.

Guitane lough, loch coiteain, lake of the little coiti or boat of oak wrought hollow, is a moraine dammed where Mangerton meets with Crohane.

Gullaba, guala, hill shoulders, hill

1,986 ft., baile Kilgarvan.

Gullane, gallan; baile in Kilcunly; pillar stone here.

Gullaun, gallan, pillar stone, baile in Kilcummin.

Gun, Gunn, Mac Giolladuinn; Wm. of Rattoo, John and David of Lyre, Hanoria of Duagh. Wm. of Lisla-hane in 1641 had Wm. of Rattoo 1699, who had Wm., who had Town-send, who had Wm. 1765, who had Townsend 1803, who had Wilson 1809, who had Hy. 1842, who had Wm. of Rattoo 1902.

Gurnett; John of Ballyrobert; Ml. of Brogue lane, Tom of John street, Ml. of Dingle had Tom, Ml., Wm., and John, and they went to U.S.A. in 1864, the brothers serving in the army there.

Gurrig island, 9acres, in Killiney.

Gurteen, goirtin, guirtin, little field; bailes in Ballinvoher, Ballynacourty, Caher, and Kilgarvan.

Gurteenavallig, goirtin a bhealaigh, baile in Kilnaughtin.

Gurteennacloona, little meadow, baile in Aghavallen.

Gurteenroe, little red field, baile in Molahiffe.

Gymnasium instruction must be a reg-ular course in the schools of Kerry.

H; uat, the white thorn tree; an auxi-liary letter in Irish language.

Habbert, Habbart, Hoibeard; Pat and and Jas. and John and Pat of Shan-talliv, Mce. of Barrow, Jas. of Knock-anish, Pat of Strand street, James of Brogue lane.

Hackett, Mac Haiceid; Martin of Firies, Pat of Tullaghna, Catherine of Lixnaw, Tom of Trippul, Pat of Cloghaneleesh, Rev. E. A. of Clogh-ane.

Hall, de Hal; David of Shelbourne street. Mrs. S. C. Hall, 1878, wrote Killarney guide book.

Hallett; Fred of Boherbee, Harold of Glanleam.

Halley, O h Ailge; Wm. of New street.

Hallidan, Julia of Faha.

Hallinan, Hy of Tonevane, Wm. of Blennerville.

Hallissey, Hallisey, Hallissy, O h Ailgeasa; 26 families in Kerry, viz.: Jas. and Ml. of Gurteen, Pat and Johanna of High street, Dan and Jerh. of Glenlough, Ml. of Drom-lusk, John of Rossdohan, Bridget of Main street, John and Andrew of Claddanure, Pat of Reen, Andrew and Jerh. of Dromore, Ml. of Maul-inagower, Dan of Gortnacurra, Mary

166

Sample page from "County Kerry Past & Present" by Jeremiah King, Mercier, 1931. The names and residences of families are thought to have been extracted from the 1901 census.

valuations, also called Cancelled Books, are organised into the Local
Government Rural and Urban districts and into Electoral divisions within each
district. These are listed in the General Alphabetic Index to Townlands of 1871.

1834

A census of the heads of household in the Catholic parishes of Prior and
Killemlagh was taken during December 1834. This census gives householders
names and numbers of males and females in each household. It is published by
de Brún, P., *A Census of the Parishes of Prior & Killemlagh*, December 1934,
JKAHS *8* (1975).

1833

A census of the heads in household for the Catholic parish of Ballyferriter taken
during January 1833. This also gives householders names and numbers of males
and females in each household. In *A Census of the Parish of Ferriter*, January
1833. JKAHS *7* (1974).

1823-1837

Tithes (a form of taxation for the upkeep of the Church of Ireland) were required
from most rural landholders of all religions. In the early part of the nineteenth
century an Act of Parliament required that the tithe be paid in money rather than
in kind as had been a custom in many areas. During the period 1823 to 1837 a
Tithe Applotment Survey was made in each civil parish to determine the value
of tithe payable by different landholders. The manuscript books of these
surveys, like the Griffith's Valuation, list the leaseholders and landowners in
each civil parish. In some parishes more than one survey was taken, while in
others the manuscript has not survived. The originals are kept at the NAI in
Dublin. Copies of Tithe Applotment Returns arranged by barony are also found
in OCM; Barony of Magunihy in vol. 7 and Barony of Trughanacmy in vol. 8.
The Special Collections Library at Samford University, Alabama (see p. 88)
has copies of all the surviving Tithe Applotment surveys for Co. Kerry.

1821

Some remnants of the 1821 Government census returns for the civil parish of
Kilcummin are to be found in the McSwiney Papers held at the RIA. The returns
have similar details to those of the 1901 and 1911 census. A copy of this material
may be viewed through the LDS.

1799

The Dublin Evening Post newspaper of July 9, 1799 includes a list of 300 prominent persons in Co. Kerry who sent a message to the Lord Lieutenant of Ireland. The name and address (parish, town or townland) of each person is given. Copies of this newspaper are available at the British Library and the NLI.

1796

During 1796, in an effort to encourage the linen industry the Irish Linen Board awarded a subsidy to farmers growing certain acreages of flax. The original list, kept at the Linen Hall Library in Belfast, contains the names of 950 persons in Co. Kerry. The list gives the name of the householder and their civil parish. In 1986 the complete list, with indexes, was published on microfiche by All-Ireland Heritage Inc., USA. A copy is also available at the NLI.

Two indexes provided with the All-Ireland Heritage microfiche organise the places mentioned, firstly by county and secondly by civil parish. The actual lists are arranged by the name of the person receiving the award. The Co. Kerry civil parishes mentioned in the microfiche are Ballinvoher, Ballinacourty, Ballyduff, Cahir, Castleisland, Clohane North, Clohane South, Coule, Dingle, Dunquin, Dunurlin, Garfiny, Inch, Kieldrum, Kielgarylander, Kielmacadir, Kielquane, Kielury, Kielflyn, Kilgobhin, Killahen, Killeyney, Kiltomey, Kinnard, Marhin,

1641-1701

The period 1640 to 1700 was a period of great change in Irish land ownership. An official record of this change is in the Books of Survey and Distribution. Shown in adjacent columns are the proprietors of land in Ireland in 1641, 1688 and 1701. Although these people are usually the wealthy, they are of interest as background to family history. Descriptions of the plots of land are also included. Several volumes of the Books have been published by the IMC but not the Co. Kerry volume. Copies of the original Books of Survey and Distribution are kept at the NAI, the NLI and the RIA in Dublin. The records for Co. Kerry appear in Volume 11 along with the records of Co.Waterford. In her book "Selection of Old Kerry Records" (see Chap. 16), Mary Hickson gives a summary of forfeited lands listed in the Books of Distribution for Co. Kerry. Her list is a summarised transcript of the original books in the NAI. Extracts from the Books of Survey and Distribution for the barony of Trughanacmy and the barony of Magunihy appear in OCM vol. 7 and vol. 1 respectively.

1659

The Census of Ireland was published in 1959 by the IMC, edited by Seamus Pender. Each county is divided into baronies, parishes and townlands. The numbers of English and Irish in each parish are given. A further column lists the tituladoes or the principal people of the parish. They are very much the well-to-do of this period in history. It is an interesting exercise to compare the spellings of townland names of a parish listed in this document with the spellings recorded in Griffith's Valuation.

1657

Several small pieces of The Civil Survey for Co. Kerry survive and are listed in an article by Pádraig de Brún in JKAHS No. 18 (1985). The civil parishes listed are Ballymacelligott, Dysart, Killemlagh, Killury, Kilmare, Ratass and Rattoo Padraig de Brún has written another article in JKAHS No. 12 (1979) on "An extract from the Civil Survey". Some other fragments of the Civil Survey in County Kerry are printed in *Analecta Hibernica* No. 24. Volume 2 of Mary Hickson's Old Kerry Records contains a list of Papist Proprietors in County Kerry given in the Civil Survey (January 27, 1656).

1622

The RSAI journal of 1924, Vol. iv, pp. 136-139, carries an article by Robert Dunlop entitled "An unpublished Survey of the Plantation of Munster in 1622". This survey is organised into counties. Six seignories in Co. Kerry are mentioned: Denis Vale (Tralee), Island of Kerry, Soflymricahill, Mullahriff, Killorglin and Ballymacdonnell. The proprietors are named, and the number of leaseholders is given. The original Ms., British Museum Mss Sloane 4756 f.80 s.q.q. portion ff88-97 relating to Munster contains the names of the leaseholders and in some cases the acreages.

1586

The Desmond Survey was taken in 1586. After the death of Gerald Fitzgerald, Earl of Desmond in 1583, the English administration at Dublin set about carving up his land with the aim of planting English colonists. To aid in this a survey of the Earl's holdings throughout Munster province was carried out. The original manuscript was burnt in the fire of 1922. Fortunately the survey has survived for two counties, Kerry and Limerick, and it gives the names of leaseholders, placenames and the sizes of the holdings.

The Co. Kerry survey is a typescript copy. It was printed in "The Kerryman" Newspaper from August through October 1927 and is also available at the NAI as MS M.5037. This manuscript and its part in Irish history is discussed by A.J. Sheehan in "Official Reaction to native Land claims in the Plantation of Munster" *Irish Historical Studies*, Vol. XXIII (92) Nov. 1983.

Chapter 5   Church Records

From 1864 the Government of Ireland required that baptisms, marriages and deaths be registered. Prior to this, Church records are an essential source of information about events such as baptisms, marriages and in some cases burials. To effectively use this chapter you should know in which civil parish(es) you believe your ancestor resided. The major denominations in Co. Kerry were Catholic and Church of Ireland, although Presbyterians and Congregationalists also worshipped in Co. Kerry.

Catholic Church Records

Baptismal and marriage records are available for all churches but unlike the Church of Ireland there are almost no Catholics records until the twentieth century. Most of the baptismal and marriage records commence in the period 1810 to 1840, the earliest being Tralee which starts in 1772.

The original parish registers are kept at the parish churches but microfilm copies (to 1880) are available for almost all Irish Catholic registers. These microfilmed copies are available at the NLI, and at many LDS libraries. However access to both original and microfilmed registers is currently restricted by the Bishop. Researchers wishing to access these records may write to the Bishop of Kerry for permission to do so. The address is Bishop's House, Killarney, Co. Kerry. Other records of the county are also being indexed. When this has been completed, a search service will be available from Killarney Genealogical Centre (see p. 86).Parish priests may search the original registers on behalf of enquirers but most cannot give priority to searching registers.

The registers of a number of Co. Kerry parishes have been published in the OCM series. The LDS has made extracts of a number of parish registers and incorporated this information into their IGI database and associated microfiche and CD-ROM set.

The following table sets out the details of the baptism (b.) and marriage (m.) entries. The table is organised by the civil parish in which the Catholic parish is situated. The reference numbers correspond to the map on p.17. Each civil parish may encompass parts of a number of Catholic parishes (see p.15 for explanation) hence the notations in the table such as "see Killarney" or "part Spa see Ardfert". The former notation means "see the entry for the civil parish of Killarney", while the latter notation means see the entry for the "Catholic parish of Spa in the civil parish of Ardfert". For each Catholic parish, details are given of the surviving records, any missing records and any other sources of copies or extracts (e.g. OCM vl. 7, IGI).

Civil Parish	Map Ref.	Catholic Parish	Period of Record	Remarks
Aghadoe	79	Fossa	b.1.1857- m.1.1858	
Aghadoe	79	Glenflesk	b.9.1821- b.1821-1875 b. 1821-1894 m.2.1831 m.1831-1848, 1853-1873, 1875-1880 m.1831-1900	Earliest IGI OCM vol. 7, 8 IGI OCM vol.7
Aghadoe	79	see also Killorglin, and Killarney		
Aghavallen	2	Ballylongford	b.3.1823- b.5.1839-10.1868 m.1826- m.3.1838-1868	 Missing Missing
Aglish	75	Firies	b/m.1.1830- b/m.1880-1900	 OCM vol. 8
Annagh	53	see Ballymacelligott or Tralee		
Ardfert	25	Ardfert	b.3.1819 b.1818-1846 b.1818-1900 m.2.1825 m.1825-1846 m.1822-1900	 IGI OCM vol. 8, 14 IGI OCM vol. 7, 8
Ardfert	25	Spa	b.11.1866- m.1.1867	
Ballincuslane	56	Knockagoshel	b/m.1850	
Ballincuslane	56	see also Brosna & Castleisland		
Ballinvoher	40	Annascaul	b.4.1829- m.5.1829- b.3.1834-3.1837	 Missing

Civil Parish	Map Ref.	Catholic Parish	Period of Record	Remarks
Ballinvoher			b.3.1839-10.1857	Missing
			m.6.1835-5.1837	Missing
			m.9.1837-9.1855	Missing
Ballinvoher	40	Ballyferriter	b.2.1807-	
			m.1.1808-	
Ballyconry	8	Ballybunion	b.11.1831-	
			m.2.1837	
Ballyduff	28	Castlegregory	b.12.1828-	
			m.2.1829	
Ballyheigue	16	Ballyheigue	b.12.1840-	
			m.1.1841-	
Ballymacelligott	49	Ballymacelligott	b/m.10.1868	
Ballinacourty	39	part Annascaul see Ballinvoher		
Ballynahaglish	45	see Ardfert		
Ballynahaglish	45	part Spa see Ardfert		
Ballyseedy	54	see Ballymacelligott		
Brosna	52	Brosna	b/m.1866-	
			b/m.1866-1875	IGI
			b.1866-1900	OCM vol. 8
			m.1872-1900	OCM vol. 8
Caher	65	Caherciveen	b/m.11.1846	
Castleisland	51	Castleisland	b.4.1823-	
			b.1823-1872	OCM vol. 4, 6
			b.1823-1872	IGI
			b.1829-1918	LDS microfilms
			m.10.1822	
			m.1822-1900	OCM vol. 7
			m.1822-1880	IGI
			m.1825-1918	LDS microfilms
Castleisland	51	part Knocknagoshel see Ballincuslane		
Castleisland	51	see Brosna		
Cloghane	27	see Dingle		
Cloghane	27	part Castlegregory see Ballyduff		
Clogherbrien	46	see Ardfert and also Tralee		
Currans	59	see Ballymacelligott and also Killeentierna		
Dingle	35	Dingle	b.2.1825-	
			m.5.1821-	
Dromod	80	Dromod	b/m.2.1850	
Duagh	15	Duagh	b.1.1819-	
			m.1.1832-	

Civil Parish	Map Ref.	Catholic Parish	Period of Record	Remarks
Duagh	15	see Listowel		
Dunquin	41	part Ballyferriter see Ballinvoher		
Dunurlin	32	part Ballyferriter see Ballinvoher		
Dysert	13	See Listowel		
Dysert	15	Lixnaw	b.8.1810	
			b.2.1845-6.1848	Missing
			m.1.1810-	
			m.6.1852-8.1856	Missing
Dysert East	61	see Killeentierna		
Fenit	44	part Spa see Ardfert		
Finuge	14	see Listowel		
Finuge	14	also part Lixnaw see Dysert		
Galey	6	see Ballyconry, also Listowel		
Garfinny	36	see Dingle		
Glanbeigh	67	Glanbeigh	b/m.3.1830-	
			b.8.1837-6.6.1841	Missing
			m. to 2.1835 only	,,
Kenmare	84	Kenmare	b/m.1.1819-	
			b.3.1824-1.1826	Missing
			m.7.1838-1.1839	,,
Kenmare	84	see also Tuosist		
Kilbonane	74	Milltown	b.10.1825	
			b.9.1840-10.1841	Missing
			m.1.1821	
			m.11.1832-10.'42	Missing
Kilcaragh	19	Lixnaw see Dysert		
Kilcaskan	87	Bonane	b/m.1846-	
Kilcolman	62	part Milltown see Kilbonane		
Kilconly	1	see Ballyconry		
Kilcredane	76	see Aglish		
Kilcrohane	82	Caherdaniel	b.2.1831-	
			m.5.1831-	
		also Sneem	b.8.1845-	
			b.11.1848-	Missing
			11.1857	
			m.2.1858-	
Kilcummin	77	Kilcummin	b.1.1821-	
		West	b.8.1859-11.1859	Missing
			b.1821-1900	OCM vol. 5
			m.1.1823-	
			m.9.1859-2.1873	Missing

Civil Parish	Map Ref.	Catholic Parish	Period of Record	Remarks
Kilcummin			m.1823-1900	OCM vol. 5
Kilcummin	77	also part Glenflesk see Aghadoe		
Kilcummin	77	also Rathmore	b.1837-	
			b.1837-1900	OCM vols. 1, 5
			m.1839-	
			m.1839-1900	OCM vols. 1, 5
Kildrum	43	see Dingle		
Kilfeighny	20	Abbeydorney	b.10.1835-	
			b.9.1844-2.1851	Missing
			m.1.1837-	
Kilfeighny	20	part Lixnaw see Dysert		
Kilflynn	24	part Abbeydorney see Kilfeighny		
Kilgarrylander	57	Castlemaine	b/m.2.1804-	
			b.7.1813-1.1815	Missing
			10.1817-4.1818	
Kilgarvan	85	Kilgarvan	b.4.1818-	
			m.11.1818-	
			m.4.1864-9.1864	Missing
Kilgobban	31	part Annascaul see Ballinvoher		
Killaha	81	part Glenflesk see Aghadoe		
Killahan	17	part Abbeydorney see Kilfeighny		
Killarney	80	Killarney	b/m.8.1792-	
			m.5.1851-1.1858	Missing
			b.1785-1900	OCM vols. 5, 6, 7, 8, 14
			b.1785-1875	LDS Exracts
			m.1792-1900	OCM vols. 5, 7
			m.1782-1800	LDS Extracts
Killarney	80	part Glenflesk see Aghadoe		
Killeentierna	60	Killeentierna	b.6.1801-	
			b.12.1809-7.1823	Missing
			b.1801-1900	OCM vols. 4, 6
			b.1801-1875	LDS Extracts
			m.6.1803-	
			m.2.1828-6.1830	Missing
			m.1803-1900	OCM vol. 6
			m.1803-1880	LDS Extracts
Killehenny	4	part Ballybunion see Ballyconry		
Killemlagh	68	see Prior		
Killinane	66	Caherciveen see Caher		
Killiney	30	part Annascaul see Ballinvoher		
Killiney	30	part Castlegregory see Ballyduff		

Civil Parish	Map Ref.	Catholic Parish	Period of Record	Remarks
Killorglin	63	Killorglin see also Glanbeigh	b/m.1886-	
Killury	11	Causeway	b.12.1782	
			b.7.1786-11.1806,	Missing
			11.1819-7.1820	
			m.2.1809-	
			m.5.1845-2.1846	Missing
Kilmoyly	22	see Ardfert		
Kilnanare	73	part Firies see Aglish		
Kilnaughtin	3	Tarbert	b/m.1859-	
Kilquane	26	part Ballyferriter see Ballinvoher		
Kilshenane	21	see Listowel		
Kinard	37	see Dingle		
Knockane	71	see Killorglin		
Knockane	71	also Tuogh	b.3.1844-	
			m.1.1843-	
Knockanure	10	part Moyvane see Murher		
Lisselton	5	part Ballybunion see Ballyconry		
Listowel	9	Listowel	b.8.1802-	
			m.1.1837-	
Marhin	33	part Ballyferriter	see Ballinvoher	
Minard	38	see Dingle		
Molahiffe	72	part Firies see Aglish		
Murhur	7	Moyvane	b.6.1831-	
			m.6.1831-*	
Nohoval	55	see Ballymacelligott		
Nohavaldaly	78	Boherbue	b.7.1833-	
			b.1833-1900	Missing
			b.12.1860-3.1863	OCM vol. 2, 11
			m.2.1863-	
			m.1863-1900	OCM vol. 11
Nohavaldaly	78	also part Rathmore see Kilcummin		
O'Brennan	30	see Ballymacelligott		
O'Dorney	23	part Abbeydorney		
Prior	69	Prior	b/m.1.1832-	
Ratass	48	see Ballymacelligott		
Ratass	48	also see Tralee		
Rattoo	12	see Killury		
Stradbally	29	see Ballyduff		
Templenoe	83	see Kenmare		

*1831-1855 not on microfilm

Civil Parish	Map Ref.	Catholic Parish	Period of Record	Remarks
Tralee	47	Tralee	b.1.1772- m.2.1774-	
Tuosist	47	Tuosist	b/m.1844-	
Valentia	64	Valentia	b.3.1825- b.7.1864-5.1867 m.2.1827- m.4.1856-1880	Missing Missing
Ventry	42	see Dingle		

Church of Ireland Parish Records

A number of the Church of Ireland registers were burnt in 1922. Those which have survived are listed in this section. The list is based on the catalogue of parish registers at the NAI, information from the Kerry Genealogical Society and DKPRI Report 22 (1895). The notation *local custody* signifies that the current church minister has the extant register or a transcript, while *none survive* denotes that the register was destroyed at some time in the past. If the records of interest are in local custody you can locate the name of the parish minister using Crockford's Clerical Directory which is available at most large reference libraries.

All of the surviving original registers are retained in local custody, except for Aghavallin, Dromod, Killury and Rattoo for which transcripts are retained locally. For the parishes of Dromod and Prior a copy of the transcript has been deposited at the NAI. For each Co. Kerry parish for which registers survive a microfilm copy is stored at the NAI for security purposes. These are not currently accessible to researchers. The RCBL, which is the official library of the controlling organisation of the Church of Ireland is gradually acquiring copies of all Co. Kerry Church of Ireland church records. Note that marriage records of the Church of Ireland churches were kept by the State from 1845 and are available in an indexed and detailed format from the RGO (see p. 87).

The Kerry Heritage Centre has indexed some records of the Church of Ireland registers that are kept in Co. Kerry. Write to the Centre (see p. 86 for address) if you wish to enquire further about this project.

Civil Parish	Map Ref.	Records Available	Where Held
Aghadoe	79	b.1842-1877	Local custody
		m.1842-1861	,,
		d.1845-1877	,,
		b/m/d. 1838-1881 approx.	NAI M5974
Aghavallen	2	m.1845-1872	Local custody
Aglish	75		None survive
Annagh	53		None survive
Ardfert	25		None survive
Ballincuslane	56		None survive
Ballinvoher	40	see Kilgobbin	
Ballyconry	8		None survive
Ballyduff	28		None survive
Ballyheige	16		None survive
Ballymacelligott	49	b/m/d.1817-1875	Local custody
		b/m/d.1817-1856	NAI MFCI 17
		"	NAI M 5991
Ballynacourty	39	b/d.1803-1877	Local custody
		m.1803-1845	,,
		see also Kilflynn	
Ballynahaglish	45		None survive
Ballyseedy	54	b.1830-1878	Local custody
		d.1831-1878	and NAI
Brosna	52		None survive
Caher	65	b. 1878-1947	RCBL
		m. 1947-76	"
Castleisland	51	b.1835-1877	Local custody
		m.1836-1876	also RCBL (parts)
		d.1836-1875	,,
Cloghane	27		None survive
Clogherbrien	46	see Ballynahaglish	
Currens	59	see Kiltallagh	
		and Ballymacelligott	
Dingle	35	b/d.1707-1875	Local custody
		m.1707-1845	,,
Dromod & Prior	70	m.1827-1842	Transcript at NAI.
		m.1822-1842	RCBL
Duagh	15		None survive
Dunquin	31	see Ventry	
Dunurlin	32		None survive
Dysert	13	see Listowel	
Dysert East	61	see Killeentierna	
Fenit	44		None survive

Civil Parish	Map Ref.	Records Available	Where Held
Finuge	14	see Listowel	
Galey	6	see Listowel	
Garfinny	36		None survive
Glanbeigh	67		None survive
Kenmare	84	b.1799-1873	Local custody
		m.1799-1845	Local custody
		d.1799-1876	"
		b.1818-1893	RCBL
		m.1819-1950	,,
		d.1818-1849	,,
Kilbonane	74	see Mollahiffe	
Kilcaragh	19	see Duagh	
Kilcolman	62		None survive
Kilconly	1	see Aghavallin	
Kilcredane	76	see Mollahiffe	
Kilcrohane		m.1846-1930	RCBL
Kilcummin	77	see Killarney	
Kildrum	43	see Ventry	
Kilfeighny	20		None survive
Kilflynn	24	b.1878-	Local custody
Kilgarrylander	57	see Kiltallagh	
Kilgarvan	58	b/m/d 1811-	Local custody
		b.1811-1850	RCBL
		m.1812-1947	"
		d.1819-1960	"
Kilgobban	31	b/m/d.1713-1754	Local custody
		b/d.1806-1875	Pub in KEP 4.1910
		m.1806-1845	and 10.1913
Killaha	81	see Kilgarvan	
Killahan	17	see Kilflynn	
Killarney	80		None survive
Killehenny	4	see Listowel	
Killemlagh	68		None survive
Killinane	66	see Cahir	
Killorglin	63	b.1840/m.1837-'40/d.1837	NAI TAB 12/63
Killury & Rattoo	11	b.1867-	Local custody
Kilmalkedar	54		None survive
Kilmoyly	22	see also Ballyheige	None survive
Kilmore		b.1826-1960	RCBL
		n.1850-1925	"
Kilnanare	73		None survive

Civil Parish	Map Ref.	Records Available	Where Held
Kilnaughtin	3	b.1785-1871 m.1785-1845 d.1786-1873	local custody and NAI MFCI 17 ,,
Kilquane	26		None survive
Kilshenane	21	see Kilflynn	
Kiltallagh	58		
Kiltomy	18	See Kilflynn	
Kinard	38		None survive
Knockane	71		None survive
Knockanure	10	see Listowel	
Liselton (Ballybunion)	5	b/d.1840-1875	Local custody NAI MFCI 17
Listowel	9	b/d.1790-1875 m.1790-1845 b.1835-72 m.1835-45/d.1836-71	Local custody NAI MFCI 17 NAI M 5970
Marhin	33	see Ventry	
Minard	38	see Kilflynn	
Molahiffe	72		None survive
Murhur	7	see Listowel	
Nohoval	55	see Ballymacelligott	
Nohavaldaly	78	b/d.1792-1877 m.1792-1847	Local custody
O'Brennan	30	see Tralee	
O'Dorney	23		None survive
Prior	69	m.1827-1842	Local custody
Ratass	48	See Tralee	
Rattoo	12	b.1868-1875 d.1870-1875 see also Killury	Local custody ,,
Stradbally	29	see Kilflynn	
Templenoe	83	see also Kilcrohane m.1849-1920	RCBL
Tralee (Blennerville)	47	b/d.1771-1875 m.1771 - 1845 b.1771-1806 to 10.1880 b.1771-1872 m.1796-1850/d.1805-1880 b.1830-1833	Local custody ,, Pub in KEP 6.1880 MAI MFC! 14 " Pub in KEP 10.1910
Tuosist	86	see Kenmare	

Civil Parish	Map Ref.	Records Available	Where Held
Valentia	64	b/d.1826-1875	LC & NAI M5988/9
Ventry	42		None survive

Other Churches

A register of the Presbyterian church in Tralee from about 1840 is retained in local custody. As early as 1820 there was a Congregationalist church in Tralee but the registers are not known to have survived.

Lists of Clergy

Information about clergymen can sometimes be useful in family research. Most Kerry families include one or two Roman Catholic priests, and there is always the possibility of a Church of Ireland clergyman in your ancestry. Then again, you might simply like to know a little more about the priest who ministered to your ancestors. The following sources list the clergy of Co. Kerry at various times in the past.

Bishops of Ardfert and Kerry 562 to 1963 are printed in OCM vol. 6. and in KEP on 22/3/1890, extracted from *Diocesan Magazine*.

Parish Priests and Curates, Currow R.C. Church 1801-1961 are printed in OCM vol. 6.

Parish Priests and Curates, Killarney and Fossa R.C. Church 1785-1805 are printed in OCM vol. 5.

Clergy Lists from Visitation Books kept at the NAI, 1669-1773 are printed in KEP 17/Nov./1875, 24/Nov./1875 and 18/Dec./1875 by Mary Agnes Hickson.

Some lists of Kerry Priests, 1750-1835 by Pádraig de Brún are printed in JKAHS, no. 18 (1985).

The Catholic Directory, Almanack and Registry has been issued annually since 1836. The Directory gives lists of parish priests and their curates within each diocese.

Irish Ecclesiastical Register was issued in the years 1817, 1818, 1824 and 1827 lists the Church of Ireland clergymen in each diocese. Each issue has an index.

Ecclesiastical Registry, by Samuel Lea in 1814. This book also lists the Church of Ireland clergymen in each diocese.

Irish Church Directory has been published annually from 1862. For each diocese the Church of Ireland clergymen in each parish are listed. An index is also provided.

Ecclesiastical Visitations

Both Catholic and Church of Ireland Bishops and Archbishops were required to periodically undertake visitations throughout the parishes in their charge. The visitations were used to collect tithes, to check on attendances, conditions of churches, report on problems and the many facets of parish life. On return a description of the visitation was often recorded. These records are of immense historical value. They record changes to parish values, leases for church land, sometimes the names of parishioners, location of churches and schools and a good deal of social history.

Many articles have been written regarding ecclesiastical visitations in Co. Kerry. The following sources are transcripts or studies of visitation records. They give an interesting background to a number of parishes in Co. Kerry and also mention prominent local persons and ministers.

Diocese of Kerry Visitations, 1615 and 1633 printed in Mary A. Hickson's *Selection of Old Kerry Records*. The information in this article is a transcript of manuscript copies at the RIA and the Trinity College Library. The visitations are those of the Church of Ireland and give the names of ministers, their parishes and occasionally some comments.

Three early nineteenth-century diocesan reports by Rev Kieran O'Shea printed in JKAHS, no.10 (1977).

Bishop Cornelius Egan's diocesan report to Rome by Rev Kieran O'Shea printed in JKAHS, no. 12 (1979).

Rev. Forster Archer's account of Kerry in 1801 by Pádraig de Brún printed in JKAHS, no. 14 (1981).

Bishop David Moriarty's Diary, 1856 by Rev Kieran O'Shea printed in JKAHS, no.17 (1984). Reverend O'Shea's article contains visitation details for a number of parishes. There are many footnotes with information on further sources to read relating to the people and places mentioned in the diary.

Rev. Daniel A. Beaufort's Tour of Kerry, 1788 by Pádraig de Brún printed in JKAHS, no. 18 (1985).

Kerry Diocese in 1890: Bishop Coffey's Survey by Pádraig de Brún, JKAS No. 22 (1989).

Converts and Qualification Rolls

At the start of the 18th century a number of Penal laws were enacted in Ireland to severely limit the rights of Catholic persons with regard to land ownership and many other areas. Some Catholics took measures to ensure they retained their rights, such as real, or nominal, conversion to the Church of Ireland or. In the late 18th century, some rights were restored to Catholics who made an oath of allegiance to the Crown. Records relating to these activities are given in the following table.

1703-1772   An Alphabetical List of Converts to Protestantism.
                  Part of Lodge's manuscripts stored at the NAI (See
                  DKPRI Report 55). Some Catholics converted or
                  "conformed" to the Protestant faith to preserve their
                  family estates. This manuscript details places of
                  residence, date of conformity and so forth.

1703-1845   Convert Rolls and Certificates of Conformities,
                  Calendars and Indexes. Stored in the NAI as records
                  from the Court of Chancery. See DKPRI Report 55.
                  These records have been indexed in "Convert Rolls"
                  by Eileen O'Byrne, IMC, Dublin, 1981.

1778-1801   Munster Province Catholic Qualification Rolls. The
                  indexes, which show the name, residence and place
                  and date of qualification, are kept at the NAI. In the
                  first of a series of acts which relaxed the Penal laws,
                  Catholics could take an oath of allegiance to the
                  Crown in return for certain rights. The records for the
                  years 1791 and 1792 are missing.

Further Reading

The following articles discuss some elements of the history of the Churches in
Co. Kerry:

Franciscan Friaries in pre-Reformation Kerry by Katherine Walsh published
    in JKAHS, no. 9 (1976).

Dr Nicholas Madgett's Constitutio Ecclesiastica, 1758 by Rev. Michael
    Manning, JKAHS, no. 9 (1976).

The Franciscan Friary, Killarney, 1860-1902, by Rev. Patrick Conlan, JKAHS,
    no. 10 (1977).

Lislaughtin Abbey by Michael McElligott, in the Kerry Archaeological
    Magazine, no. 21 (1912/14).

David Moriarty (1814-77) by Rev. Kieran O'Shea printed in numbers 3 to 6 of
    JKAHS under the sub-headings of "The Making of a Bishop; Reforming a
    Diocese; Politics and Ecclesiastical Affairs".

Bonaventure O'Connor Kerry: A seventeenth-century Franciscan abroad by
    Rev. Cathaldus Giblin, JKAHS, no. 17 (1984).

Chapter 6   Civil Registration

From 1845 marriages conducted in the Church of Ireland were registered by the State. In 1864 registration was expanded to include all births, marriages and deaths in Ireland. This requirement, known as Civil Registration, is the major source of family vital statistics for the period 1864 to date.

The records of Irish Civil Registration are kept at the Registrar-Generals Office (RGO) in Dublin as well as various other sources (see p. 42). The records from 1845 have been indexed (yearly to 1878, and quarterly from that year.) Each index is sorted alphabetically by surname and gives the Registration District in which the event occurred and the reference number to the registration volume and page.

How useful are the Civil Registration records if your ancestor if known to have emigrated from Ireland before 1864? Firstly there is the possibility of other relatives remaining in Ireland and being recorded in the registers. Secondly, the parents of many Irish emigrants died in Ireland. If they died after 1863 their death certificate should be obtainable. This is valuable information since it may provide a specific address of the family home.

The Civil Registration records contain the following relevant information:

Births

Surname, Given Name, Date and Place of birth, Fathers Name and Occupation, Mothers Name and Maiden Name, and details of the informant (i.e. name and association with child).

Marriage

Parish and Church in which marriage was conducted, Date, Names, Ages (usually only "full age", or "minor"), Marital Status, Occupations and Residences of Bride and Groom; Names and Occupations of the Fathers of the couple; and names of Witnesses.

Deaths

Surname, Given Name, Date and Place of Death, Age, Occupation, Cause of Death and Details of Informant.

The Civil Registration records are available from several sources, which are listed below.

Registrar General's Office, 8/11 Lombard Street, Dublin 2

The indexes may be viewed at the RGO search room in Dublin by paying a daily search fee. If you locate a relevant index entry a photocopy or a certified copy of the entry can be obtained on the day by payment of further fees. The record books may not be searched personally. You may also write to the Registrar-General in Dublin to request a search. The RGO will only search ONE five year period for a particular event. If a likely entry is found you will be sent the details with the option to purchase the certificate if you believe it is the correct entry.

Libraries of Church of Jesus Christ of Latter-Day Saints

The LDS has microfilm copies of Civil Registration indexes for the whole of the Republic of Ireland. The Birth index microfilms have about one year per film, Marriages about three years per film and Deaths about two years per film. The microfilms cover the years 1864 to 1958. There are no separate indexes for Co. Kerry. The LDS have extracted some of the information in the Civil Registration records (births and marriages) and placed it in the 1988 IGI. For Co. Kerry they have extracted records for the period 1864 to 1866 (approximately), although this varies in each parish.

Published Sources

Some Civil Registration records for Co. Kerry have been printed in OCM. Births in the barony of Trughanacmy 1864 to 1869, are printed in OCM vols. 5 and 7. Marriages for the Trughanacmy barony 1845 to 1900 are printed in OCM vols. 4 and 5. Marriages for the barony of Magunihy 1871 to 1900, are printed in OCM vol. 5.

Chapter 7   Commercial & Social Directories

Directories are useful for locating ancestors, especially wealthy landowners or "gentry", clergy, the wealthier farmers and a multitude of town and village shoemakers, coopers, grocers, teachers and professionals. In the late 1890's the names of residents of Kerry towns and some villages are given in directories for Co. Kerry.

How useful are directories in genealogy? For ancestors who were town folk and worked at a trade the directories provide a means of locating them and their trade or profession. Such information is not available from Griffith's Valuation. Directories are also useful as a means of determining how your ancestor's home town grew (or shrunk) over time.

Two different series of directories were published containing information on Co. Kerry towns. They were Pigot's (later known as Slater's), and Guy's. These directories are all available in the NLI and may also be available in your regional library (see p. 85 for addresses). The coverage of these directories is shown in the table on the following page. The top of the table lists the towns specifically mentioned in each directory. The lower half of the table shows the coverage of the directory (i.e. which social classes are included, the basis of geographical organization etc.) to help further explain the contents of each directory. An 'X' in a particular cell of the table indicates that the town or the category is to be found in the directory.

Directory Name and Year								
	Pigot	Slater				Guy's		Slater
	1824	'46	'56	'70	'81	'86*	'93*	1894
Town								
Ballylongford				x	x	x	x	x
Caherciveen			x	x	x	x	x	x
Castleisland		x	x	x	x	x	x	x
Castlemaine				x	x	x	x	x
Dingle	x	x	x	x	x	x	x	x
Kenmare	x	x	x	x	x	x	x	x
Killarney	x	x	x	x	x	x	x	x
Listowel	x	x	x	x	x	x	x	x
Milltown		x	x	x	x	x	x	x
Tarbert	x	x	x	x	x	x	x	x
Tralee	x	x	x	x	x	x	x	x
Valentia		x	x	x	x	x	x	x
Category								
Gentry	x	x	x	x	x	x	x	x
Nobility	x	x	x	x	x	x	x	x
Clergy	x	x	x	x	x	x	x	x
Traders	x	x	x	x	x	x	x	x
Farmers				x	x	x	x	x
Police								x
Index to All								
Co. Kerry Residents			x	x				
Organised by:								
Postal District			x			x		
Parish			x	x	x	x		

The full names of the above directories are:

1824   J. Pigot's, *City of Dublin & Hibernian Provincial Directory*

1846   Slater's, *National Commercial Directory of Ireland*

1856   Slater's, *Royal National Commercial Directory of Ireland*

1870   Slater's, *Directory of Ireland*

1881   Slater's, *Royal National Commercial Directory of Ireland*

*1886   Francis Guy's, *Postal Directory of Munster*" This was issued annually from 1889. This also has listings from a large number of the villages surrounding the larger centres.

1893   Francis Guy's, *Directory of Munster*

1894   Slater's, *Royal National Directory of Ireland*

Chapter 8   Wills & Administrations

Wills are documents created by persons to record their instructions for disposal of property (estate) after their death. Probate is the process by which a court declares the will to be legally valid and by which the executor is appointed to execute the instructions of the will. If a person died intestate, that is without making a will, the court (see below) decided on the disposal of the deceased's property and the resulting document determining the decision is called an administration. They then appointed an administrator, usually a relative or close friend, to dispose of the estate according to their decision. These administrators would commonly lodge a bond (i.e. money) as surety that they would do so, hence Administrative Bonds.

Prior to 1858 the Church of Ireland administered the probate system in Ireland. Each diocese had its own court, called a Diocesan or Consistorial Court. The whole of Co. Kerry is covered by the diocese of Ardfert and Aghadoe except for the civil parish of Kilcaskan, which is part of the diocese of Ross. If estate left by a deceased had worth of greater than five pounds in a second diocese then probate was granted by a central court known as the Prerogative Court of Armagh.

After 1858 the administration of probate in Ireland shifted from the Church courts to Civil courts. Probate Registries were created. County Kerry is covered by two different Probate Registries from 1858 to 1965. The baronies of Clanmaurice and Iraghticonnor are part of the Limerick District Registry. The remainder of Co. Kerry is part of the Cork District Registry. The original wills, and transcripts of the District Registry rulings, were sent to the Principal Registry Office in Dublin periodically. Most of the 19th century Principal Registry material was destroyed in the fire of 1922, however some transcripts retained by the District Registries have survived.

Wills and Administrations are extremely valuable for ancestral research. Both document types may contain details on family members and their relationships, property ownership and occupations. The researcher must consider the economic circumstances of their ancestor at the time of death. For the pre-1858 period a very wealthy ancestor or an ancestor living on a diocesan border who had property across that border might have left a Prerogative will.

Other residents of Co. Kerry would most likely have dealt with the Diocesan or Consistorial Court. From 1858 the researcher must consider in which part of Co. Kerry the ancestor resided to determine which District Registry applies. If the surviving records of any of the courts do not contain a relevant document, the final two sections of this chapter list some collections of transcripts and other material that may prove useful. In particular the extracts and indexes made by the Commissioners for Inland Revenue in England and those held by the Registry of Deeds (see p. 50) are of use.

Prerogative Court of Armagh (pre-1858)

The original wills of this Court were destroyed in the PRO fire but various transcripts and indexes have survived. The most useful of these is the Betham material. Sir William Betham, the Ulster King at Arms, spent a good deal of time in the early nineteenth century indexing and abstracting the records of the Prerogative Court. The Abstracts contain the genealogical information contained in each will or administration and they are therefore very valuable to the family historian. Prerogative indexes simply list the name of the deceased, with date of death and/or date of probate. Part of this index has been published in Index to Prerogative Wills of Ireland 1538-1810 by Sir Arthur Vicars. The following table lists the available Prerogative Court material.

Document Type	Time Frame	Location	Remarks
Will Index	1536-1858	NAI	Index prepared by Sir W. Betham.
		LDS	Microfilm copies of above.
	1538-1810	Pub.	Published as Index to the Prerogative Wills of Ireland by Sir Arthur Vicars, Dublin 1897, reprinted in OCM vol. 6.
Will Abstracts	1536-1802	NAI	Betham Abstracts.
Will Pedigrees	1536-1802	NAI	Sir W. Betham created brief family trees from the information in his abstracts.
		LDS	Microfilm copy of pedigrees.
Will Books	1664-68	NAI	Will Books contain transcripts of the proved wills. Indexed in the NAI Card Index to Testamentary Records.
	1706-8 (A-W)		
	1726-9 (A-W)		
	1777 (A-L)		
	1813 (K-Z)		
	1834 (A-E)		
Admin Grants Index	1595-1810	OCM	Vol. 4
Admin Abstracts	1595-1802	NAI	Prepared by Sir W. Betham.

Consistorial Court of Ardfert and Aghadoe (pre. 1858)

If the estate of the deceased did not exceed five pounds in a second diocese the will or administration was dealt with by the Diocesan or Consistorial Court. The records of the court of the diocese of Ardfert and Aghadoe were mostly destroyed. All that remains are indexes which state the name of the deceased, place of residence, title (e.g Rev.), sometimes occupation and the year in which probate was granted.

Document Type	Time Frame	Location	Remarks
Will Indexes	1690-1800	Pub.	Printed by Phillimore and Thrift, London in 1913. Reprinted by Baltimore Genealogical Publishing Co. in 1970.
	1690-1858	OCM	Vol. 5.
Admin Indexes	1782-1858	OCM	Vol. 5.
Admin Indexes	1737-1837	NAI	Included with records for the Courts of Clonfert, Killala, Achonry and Limerick.

Consistorial Court of Cork and Ross (pre. 1858)

The civil parish of Kilcaskan is part of the Cork and Ross Diocese. The records of the court of the diocese of Ross were mostly burnt in the PRO fire. All that remains are indexes which state the name of the deceased, place of residence, title (e.g Rev.), sometimes occupation and the year in which probate was granted.

Document Type	Time Frame	Location	Description
Will Indexes	1548-1800	Pub.	Ed. by G. Thrift; pub. by Phillimore and Thrift, London in 1913. Reprinted by Genealogical Publishing Co., Baltimore in 1970.
	1548-1858	OCM	Vol. 8.
	1548-1833	Pub.	Journal of Cork Historical and Archaeological Society, 1895-1898.
Admin Indexes	1612-1858	OCM	Vol. 6.

Principal Probate Registry Records (1858-)

Probates were also recorded at a central registry known as the Principal Registry which is situated in Dublin. Theoretically all wills proved in the District Registries were also registered in Dublin. In practice this was not done and furthermore not all the wills proved in each registry were summarised in the District Registry will books. Most wills proved since 1858 have survived in some form. What has survived is detailed in the following table.

Document Type	Time Frame	Location	Remarks
Will Books	1874	NAI	Surnames G to M
	1878		All Names
	1891		Surnames G to M
	1896		Surnames A to F
Admin Grant	1878,1883,	NAI	
Books	1891,1893,		
	1904-1960		
Index to Unproved	1858-1899	NAI	
Wills	1904-1960		

Most Will and Administration material from the Principal Registry (post 1904) and District Registries (post 1900) is available at the NAI. This material has been indexed into Calendars, consolidated from 1858 to 1877 into a single volume. There are four volumes per year for the post 1877 indexes. The Calendars are available in the NAI search room.

Limerick District Probate Registry (1858-)

The Limerick District Probate Registry includes the baronies of Iraghticonnor and Clanmaurice in the North of County Kerry. A reasonable number of the Will books have survived for this period although they do not necessarily contain all of the wills proved in each year.

Document Type	Time Frame	Location	Remarks
Original Wills	1900-1960	NAI	
Will Books	1858-1900	NAI	
	(7 vols)	OCM	Printed in vols. 11, 14.
	1858-1888	LDS	Microfilm of NAI Holdings
Probate Grant	1858-1868,	NAI	
Books	1873-1877,		
	1899-1960		
Admin Grant	1858-1864,	NAI	
Books	1899-1960		
Will and Admin	1900-1917,	NAI	
Indexes	1928		

Cork District Probate Registry (1858-)

The Cork District Probate Registry includes all of County Kerry south of the Barony of Clanmaurice. More of the Cork District Will books have survived for this district than for the Limerick District. Much of the material may be consulted in the NAI and the Co. Kerry material is also transcribed in OCM.

Document Type	Time Frame	Location	Remarks
Original Wills	1900-1960	NAI	
Will Books	1858-1900	NAI	
		OCM	Vols 11, 14.
Probate Grant	1858-1869	NAI	
Books	1898-1960	NAI	
Admin Grant	1858-1891	NAI	Vols 11,14.
Books (with	1895-1960	OCM	
Will annexed)			
Admin Grant	1858-1869	NAI	
Books	1898-1960		
Indexes of Wills,	1874-1879	NAI	
Administrations	1897 (incomplete)		
	1898-1899		
	1900-1960		

County Kerry Crown and Peace Records

After 1922 documents from the Co. Kerry Clerk of the Crown and Peace were transferred to the NAI. These documents include various will and administration papers. The documents are of some genealogical value, but it would be advisable to start with the Principal and District registry records first, as there are no indexes to the documents listed in the following table.

Document Type	Time Frame	Location
Civil Bill Book (Testamentary)	Trinity 1873-11 January 1904	NAI
	August 1904-June 1914 July 1914-1932	
Probate and Admin Papers	1894, 1898, 1899-1913, 1917-1921, 1924	NAI

Other Sources

Certain individuals and organisations have, for many different reasons, made transcripts of Irish wills and administrations. The following table details a number of useful sources for such transcripts.

Document Type	Time Frame	Where Held	Remarks
Will and Admin Registers	1828-1839 Part of 1834 missing.	NAI	The Commissioners of Inland Revenue, London; transcripts of Irish Will and Admin Registers in their collection.
Will and Admin Indexes	1828-1879	NAI	The Commissioners of Inland Revenue, London; indexes to Irish Will and Admin Registers.
Inquisitions Post-Mortem	1563-1700	Pub.	Records for Connaught and Munster in Public Records of Ireland, supplement to the 8th Report, 1819: name, county and date are given.
		OCM	Printed in vol. 14.
Will and Admin. Transcripts	1528-1859	RCBL	The W.H. Welply collection contains some Munster items.
		OCM	Munster items are printed in vol. 14.
Registered Wills	1708-1745(i) 1746-1788(ii) 1785-1832(iii)	Pub.	Registry of Deeds, Dublin, Abstracts of Wills, vols i and ii, edited by P.B. Eustace,

			IMC, Dublin, (1954-56), vol. iii edited by P.B. Eustace and E.Ellis, IMC, Dublin, (1984).
Will Abstracts	various	RIA	The MacSwiney Papers

Chapter 9   Memorial Inscriptions

Memorial inscriptions include tombstones and inscriptions, either as memorials, or to mark the burial place of a person. Most cemetery gravestones have not been transcribed which is a pity because registers of burials for Catholic parishes do not start until the twentieth century.

The graves of the vast majority of the peasantry were not marked in any permanent way. Gravestones or other memorials will usually only exist for those who could afford permanent headstones. However, memorials will often mention several generations of a family and therefore the gravestone of even a remote relative may be useful to the family historian.

Printed Memorial Inscriptions

The following table lists known transcripts of Co. Kerry Memorial inscriptions within each civil parish. Both Catholic and Protestant sites are listed in the same table because Catholics were sometimes buried in Protestant graveyards because there was no Catholic graveyard available and vice versa. Therefore the researcher should check all graveyards in an area of interest. In this table Catholic graveyards and churches are marked RC, the Church of Ireland graveyards are marked CoI. Churches without an RC or CoI designation signify that the ownership of the site is not specific to one church, or not specifically mentioned in the transcript source. The transcripts which have Finuge Heritage Society as the source are available from the Society (see p. 85 for address).

Civil Parish	Place	Source
Aghadoe	Aghadoe (RC)	OCM vol. 6.
	Barraduff (RC)	OCM vol. 6.
	Church of Sacred Heart (RC)	OCM vol. 6.
	Aghadoe (CoI)	OCM vol. 6.
Aghavallin	Lislaughtin Abbey (RC)	Full transcript held by Kerry Genealogical Society. Partial transcript (surname O'Connor) is given in this chapter.

Civil Parish	Place	Source
	Aghavallin(CoI)	Kerry Genealogical Society.
Aglish	Firies (RC)	OCM vol. 6.
Ardfert	Ardfert (RC)	OCM vol. 8.
	Ardfert Abbey	Kilk.Arch.Soc. Transcripts ii (1852-3) pp. 128-133
Ballymacelligott	Ballymacelligott (RC)	OCM vol. 8, 11.
Brosna	Brosna Cemetery (RC)	OCM vol. 6
	Brosna Church (RC)	OCM vol. 6
Caherciveen	Killevanogue (RC)	NAI: 57 inscriptions.
	Marian Place (RC)	NAI: 5 inscriptions.
Castleisland	Dysert (RC)	OCM vol. 6.
	Kilbannivane (RC)	OCM vol. 6.
	Kilmurry (RC)	OCM vol. 6.
	Castleisland (CoI)	OCM vol. 6.
Clogherbrien	Clogherbrien (RC)	OCM vol. 8.
Currens	Currens(RC)	OCM vol. 6.
	Ardcrone	OCM vol. 6.
Dingle	Dingle (RC)	JAPMD.
	Rahennyhooig (RC)	NAI: 49 inscriptions.
	Dingle	Kilk.Arch.Soc. Transcripts ii (1852-3) pp. 128-133
Duagh	St. Brigid's Cemetery (RC)	OCM vol. 8.
	St. Brigid's Church (RC)	OCM vol. 8.
	Duagh (RC)	OCM vol. 11.
	Duagh	Finuge Heritage Society
Dysert East	Kilsarcon Cemetery (RC)	OCM vol. 6.
Finuge	Finuge (RC)	A *Span Across Time* by the Finuge Heritage Society shows plot locations and surnames. The Finuge Heritage Society holds further details.
Garfinny	Garfinny (RC)	JAPMD and JSK
	Garfinny	Kilk.Arch.Soc. Transcripts ii (1842-3) pp. 128-133
Galey	Galey	Finuge Heritage Society
Kilcummin	St. Agatha's (RC)	OCM vol. 6.
	Glenflesk (RC)	OCM vol. 6.
	Gneeveguilla (RC)	OCM vol. 6.
	Kilcummin (RC)	OCM vol. 6.
	Rathmore (RC)	OCM vol. 6.
Killarney	Rathmore (old) (RC)	OCM vol. 6.
	Fossa Cemetery (RC)	OCM vol. 6.

SELECTIONS

FROM

OLD KERRY RECORDS,

Historical and Genealogical,

WITH

INTRODUCTORY MEMOIR, NOTES, AND APPENDIX.

BY

MARY AGNES HICKSON.

London

PRINTED BY WATSON & HAZELL,
28, CHARLES STREET, HATTON GARDEN.

1872.

Civil Parish	Place	Source
	Fossa Church (RC)	OCM vol. 6.
	Muckross Abbey (RC)	OCM vol. 6.
	New Cemetery (RC)	OCM vol. 6.
	RC Cathedral (RC)	OCM vol. 6.
	Killarney (CoI)	OCM vol. 6.
Kilmurry	Kilmurry (RC)	JAPMD and JSK
Kilnanare	Kilnanare (RC)	OCM vol. 6.
Killeentierna	Cordal (RC)	OCM vol. 6.
	Currans (RC)	OCM vol. 6.
	Killeentierna (RC)	OCM vol. 6.
	Molahiffe (RC)	OCM vol. 6.
Killeheny	Ballybunion (RC)	OCM vol. 11.
Killorglin	Killorglin (RC)	OCM vol. 8, 11.
Kilnanare	Kilnanare	Finuge Heritage Society
Kilquane	Kilquane (RC)	OCM vol. 6.
Kiltomey	Kiltomey (RC)	JAPMD
	Kiltomey Church	Kilk.Arch.Soc. Transcripts ii (1852-3) pp. 128-133
Lisselton	Lisselton (RC)	JAPMD
Listowel	Listowel (RC)	OCM vol. 11.
	St.Johns Church (CoI)	OCM vol. 8.
Murher	Murher (RC)	Kerry Genealogical Society.
Nohoval	Nohoval (RC)	OCM vol. 6, 8, 11.
O'Brennan	O'Brennan (RC)	OCM vol. 8, 11.
Tralee	Spa (RC)	OCM vol. 11.
	Tralee (RC)	OCM vol. 8, 11.
	Tralee Abbey (RC)	JAPMD
Ventry	Ventry (CoI)	Kilk.Arch.Soc. Trasncripts ii (1852-3) pp. 128-133

Miscellaneous Transcriptions

There are several uncatalogued transcripts of Co. Kerry graveyard and church transcripts. The *M.R. Lascelles-Kelly* manuscript of monumental inscriptions in seven counties including Co. Kerry is available on LDS Film 0100153 (item 1) and LDS Film 0100219 (item 1). *Miscellaneous Transcriptions and Epitaphs* are given in a chapter of the same name in Mary Agnes Hickson's *Selections of Old Kerry Records*, Vol. 1, p. 250. A few old inscriptions picked up through Kerry was published in The Kerry Magazine vol. 3, no. 35, pp. 174-176, Nov 1, 1856. Kerry Mortuary Inscriptions are to be found in the Kerry Archaeological Magazine vol. 4, pp. 199-204, Oct 1917. The Association for Preservation of Memorials of the Dead in Ireland has transcribed tombstones from various sources. The transcripts, published in their Journal are indexed by name and therefore easily accessed.

Cemetery Transcription

A collection of O'Connor headstones from Lislaughtin Abbey, Aghavallen parish in North Kerry, were transcribed by Dr. Kate Hammond and Dr. Louise Prentice in 1988.

The transcript illustrates the type of information you can expect to find from cemetery inscriptions. You will note that it is not particularly voluminous, but it may be all that is recorded about your ancestor. I have removed all post-1955 headstones from the transcript for the purpose of privacy and as a mark of respect to the local people.

Aghavallen Parish - Lislaughtin Abbey Cemetery Transcripts

Anne, relict of the late John O'Connor of Ahanegar, died Mar 8, 1892

James M O'Connor, Tarbert, died Dec 13, 1916 aged 72

Faded headstone,"Erected for Mary McMahon, died 6 Oct 1919, aged 72
    brother Patrick O'Connor died 24 Sept 1876 aged 24

Patrick O'Connor, Ballymaghes, died 6 October 1908, aged 77
    wife Johanna - no details given.

Patrick O'Connor, Asdee, died 1921
    his wife Jane, died 1941
    his son Dennis,
    also, Johanna and Bartholemew (no details given)

Jeremiah O'Connor, died February 27, 1873, aged 57

Mary O'Connor, died 25 June 1890, aged 11

James O'Connor, Tarbert, died 13 Dec 1916, aged 72

Johanna Rice (nee O'Connor), died 14 Mar 1936

Richard O'Connor, died 31 May 1768, aged 32

Anne O'Sullivan (nee O'Connor), died 5 Apr 1871, aged 56. Erected by her son James O'Sullivan, Chicago, USA

Margaret O'Connor, Kilcolgan, died 13 Dec 1919, aged 74

Joseph O'Connor, died 24 Oct 1949

If the cemetery you are looking for is not listed in this chapter then you must make a local visit to see for yourself. Use the Ordnance Survey maps described in the chapter on Maps to locate all the churches, chapels and graveyards in the parish. Griffith's Valuation is also good for this purpose. If you do visit the cemetery note down as many headstones as you can. Send a copy of your notes to the NAI, the KCL or have them published in a journal so that others may make use of your work.

Chapter 10   Land Tenure and Ownership

Records relating to the tenure and ownership of land are a useful source for family history researchers. In Co. Kerry various estate (land) owners and government institutions such as the Irish Land Commission have created these records at various times from the 17th century. Much of this material covers the 19th and 20th centuries. The Registry of Deeds in Dublin, the Irish Land Commission, the NLI and the NAI all have collections of land tenure and ownership records. The details of each of their record holdings are discussed in this chapter. See the notes on Griffith's Valuation on p. 22.

Registry of Deeds

The Registry of Deeds was begun in 1708. Agreements between parties, i.e. deeds, were registered as legal documents so that there was an established record. The majority of these deeds relate to land transactions such as sales, mortgages and leases. They can be extraordinarily detailed in regard to the families of the parties involved, particularly where they deal with agreements within families. Marriage agreements, and agreements relating to wills, were also registered. Although the number of deeds registered for Co. Kerry is relatively few in comparison to other counties, it is nevertheless a useful source.

There are two indexes to the records in the Registry of Deeds; the surname index and the placename index. Having found a particular item of interest in the index, you can then view a transcript (detailed summary) of the Deed. The originals are also kept at the Registry but are not generally consulted by researchers. However, copies can be purchased. All Index volumes are available on microfilm from the LDS.

Researchers should take care when searching the Index volumes for the Registry of Deeds. The indexes are sorted by the name of the grantor, not by the name of the grantee. Only the first name mentioned on the Deed is usually listed in the index. A cursory search of the index might lead you to the erroneous conclusion that there are no deeds for your ancestor. My advice is to start with the place name index, armed with a list of the townlands in which you believe your ancestor to have resided at a particular date. The other option is to use the

Name Index using a list of the known landowners in the parish or area you are searching.

A separate index to some records of the Registry of Deeds, i.e. Demises of land 1726-1798 for Co. Kerry, researched by M.A.Hickson, was printed in KEP of November 6th and 10th, 1875.

Estate Records

Throughout the last five hundred years wealthy land owners have controlled various large tracts of land in Co. Kerry, usually referred to as estates. These estates were sub-leased as smaller estates or as individual farms, or rented in small holdings. Most estates, whether they were managed in person by the landlord or by an agent, generated many documents. These generally include rent rolls, ledgers, correspondence, deeds and estate maps. Being private documents, estate records are not required to be stored in public record offices. The NAI and the NLI hold major collections of Co. Kerry estate records, while further records are still retained privately.

It is worth finding out the major estate owners in the parish from which your ancestors originated as this will help to determine if any relevant estate or family papers survive. Griffith's Valuation (p. 22) provides one such list of land lessors. Other sources for estate owners' names include Commercial and Social Directories (p. 43), local histories (p. 85) and Samuel Lewis's "Topographical Dictionary of Ireland" (1837).

Some of the major collections of Estate Records for Co. Kerry are listed in the following table. One of the major collections of Co. Kerry estate records, those of the Earl of Kenmare, are useful as an insight into estate life in Co. Kerry in the 18th and 19th centuries.

Estate Owner	Place and Years of Holding	Document details
Earl of Kenmare (Browne)	Kenmare, Barony of Dunkerron (1620-date)	(1)The Kenmare Manuscripts, published by IMC, 1942. Includes rental books, letters and estate notebooks. (2)Estate Ledgers (1724-1731,1740-1826) pub. in OCM vols. 7 and 9. (3)Rentals (1705-1864) pub. in OCM vols. 6 and 9. (4)Acreages (1721) pub. in OCM vol. 9.

Estate Owner	Place and Years of Holding	Document details
		(5)Lord Kenmare's Private Notebook (1755-1757) pub. in OCM vol. 9. (6)Maps of Townlands in the Kenmare Estate (1720-1725) pub. in OCM vol. 7.
Bateman	Oak Park, Barony of Trughanacmy (1697-)	About 500 items, mainly deeds and leases for this estate are mentioned in DKPRI Report 58, p. 28.
Godfrey	Kilcolman parish, and locale Estate and family deeds (324), 1677-1858.	JKAJHS 20-23 (1987-90).
Locke	18th century.	NLI: holds a collection of estate papers, surveys, valuations, rentals and maps (1762-1765) for the Locke Estate in the 19th century.
Sandes	Aghavallin, Kilnaughtin, Murher Civil Parishes, Barony of Iraghticonnor, 1680-1920.	NLI Ms.1792 is a rental for estates of Thomas W. Sandes, Sallowglen (1792-1828). The rental gives the names of the tenants, townland, details of tenure agreement and lists of payments made for the tenure. Index at front of volume. NLI has other records of the Sandes estates but they are not catalogued.
Trant	Dingle, Barony of Corkaguiny.	Two maps of the Trant estate in Co. Kerry, dated 1799 are kept at the NLI.

The following journal articles about various estates in Co. Kerry supplement the information in the table.

Landlord-tenant relations of the Shelburne Estate, in "Kenmare, Bonane and Tuosist", 1770-75 by Gerard J. Lyne in JKAHS no. 12 (1979) includes the 1773 rentals of 46 holdings plus notes on families of Orpen, Petty, Lyne, MacFinin Duibh and O'Sullivan.

Land Tenure in Kenmare and Tuosist 1696 - c.1716, by Gerard J. Lyne, printed
   in JKAHS, no. 10 (1977). As well as discussing the tenure Lyne gives lists
   of tenants and notes on them (lands rented, rents, obligations).
Land Tenure in Kenmare 1720-1770, by Gerard J. Lyne printed in JKAHS, No.
   11 (1978). Continues on from his article in Number 10 of JKAHS. Includes
   some tenant renewal lists.

Family Land Ownership/Tenure Records

Collections of documents pertaining to the land ownership or tenure of several
Co. Kerry families have survived. They may be used to trace a particular family
over a long period of time.

Family Name	Place and Time	Description
Blennerhassett and Marshall	Co. Kerry, (1713-1870)	The NAI holds 63 documents dating from 1713 - 1870 including 36 deeds.
Herbert	Cahirnane and Muckross 1669-1859	DKPRI, Report 58, p. 38 lists a collection of testamentary documents, deeds and miscellaneous papers dating 1669 to 1859.
McGillicuddy	The Reeks	The McGillicuddy Papers , by W. Maziere-Brady, Longmans, Green and Co., London, 1867.
McMahon, Neligan and Munsell families Castleisland parish.		Deeds, Leases, Settlements, Mortgages and other documents for these families extracted from the Castleisland R.C. parish register - LDS film 1279379.
Raymond	Ballyloughran 1663-1824	NAI holds 14 deeds for this family and their land ownership in Co. Kerry.
Lord Monteagle (Spring)		The NAI holds a collection of 290 documents dating 1669 to 1925 relating to the Spring and allied Rice families and their properties in Co. Kerry and Co. Limerick.

Incumbered Estate Records

From 1849 to 1904 the Incumbered Estates Board, later called the Landed Estates Court, worked to facilitate the transfer of bankrupt estates to solvent owners. Many estate owners were bankrupted due to the economic situation in the 1830's-60's. Their records are now in the NAI. The NAI holdings are listed in DKPRI, Report 55, Appendix vi. They include Conveyance Records for 1850-1881 and 1892-1901. Pre-1860 rentals for Incumbered Estates in Co. Kerry are available from the LDS on microfilms 0258820 and 0258821, which are copies of the originals in the NLI. Some of the Incumbered Estates, and Landed Estates, Court records are in the possession of the Irish Land Commission (see below).

Irish Land Commission

The Irish Land Commission was instituted in 1881, with the initial purpose of repairing the imbalance in rent values across Ireland. The ILC gained greater scope in the next thirty years, and the power to purchase and break-up the estates. The Congested Districts Board (CDB) was instituted in 1891 to assist relocation of persons from areas of overcrowding, which included all of Co. Kerry. The CDB was merged into the ILC in 1923.

The records held by the ILC are of three different types. The first type are *Historic Records of some estates* which came under the ruling of the Landed Estates and Incumbered Estates Court and were also affected by the ILC. The second type are *Records of Ownership of Properties* from the 1880's to the present day. Finally there are *Records of the Congested Districts Board*, including Inspectors reports and other details of the Board's work. The holdings of the ILC are catalogued in the Keane Catalog (sorted by Barony), a copy of which is available in the NLI reading room. The following table gives an example of Co. Kerry records listed in the Keane catalog.

Reference	Estate Name	Records
Box 135 (LC33)	Thomas W. Sandes, Iraghticonnor, Co. Kerry	Four Incumbered Estates Court conveyances with rental 1856. Deeds (20) 1856 - 1886: Names of Parties listed. Sandes family pedigree 1799+
EC 3890	Maxwell V.Blacker-Douglas,Larha, Aghavallen parish, Iraghticonnor barony.	Landed Estates Court conveyance with rental 1874.Deeds (2) 1872, 1875.

The records of the ILC are useful to family history researchers for two reasons.

The historic records (see previous table) fill some gaps in the records for the 19th century. The post 1880 records are useful for tracing the ownership of a particular property to the present day. To do so you must first acquire the folio number of that property from the Land Registry in Dublin (see p. 85) before applying to the ILC. The ILC records are organised by property rather than owner hence the requirement for the Folio number. Both the ILC and Land Registry are concerned with current land conveyancing (transfer of ownership) and must give historic research work a lower priority. The name of the townland and owner is the least amount of information required by the Land Registry when providing Folio numbers. Where possible the property should be identified on a map such as a Griffiths Valuation map (see p. 22).

Chapter 11   Newspapers

Newspapers have an interesting history in Co. Kerry. About twenty different papers have begun publishing at different periods, in Co. Kerry, most of them in the early nineteenth century. The earliest is the Kerry Evening Post which was first published in 1771. The extent to which copies survive varies. Major collections are available at the British Library, and the National Library of Ireland. The Kerry County Library has microfilm copies of most of the material. This chapter also lists extracts from newspapers printed outside Co. Kerry which contain notices mentioning Co. Kerry persons.

Much work has been done to index and abstract the biographical notices appearing in Co. Kerry newspapers. OCM contains the major source of newspaper extracts. This is not to suggest that the original newspapers have no value. Various advertisements, court reports, articles of historical events and news reporting may be used to gather information about an ancestor. The following table lists Co. Kerry newspapers, the place and years of publication, details of major collections, and of the abstracts and indexes made from these collections.

Newspaper Publication	Publishing D etails	Where Held	Time Frame	Notes
Kerry Evening Post	Tralee 1774-1917	NLI	1813-24 1828-1917	Incomplete BL,KCL
		BL, KCL	1813-1824 1828-1917	Incomplete
		OCM	1828 - 1864	vol. 6 (Indexes)
		OCM	1864 - 1872	vol. 11 (Indexes)
		OCM	1874 - 1902	vol. 11 (Indexes)
		OCM	1903 - 1917	vol. 15 (Indexes)
		CUL	March 20, 1793	(vol. V. no. 25)
		RIA	1850-1917	Nine volumes of articles about Co. Kerry families; Part of Fuller papers.

Newspaper Publication	Publishing Details	Where Held	Time Frame	Notes
Chute's Western Herald (Western Herald from 1828)	Tralee 1791-1835	NLI	1791-1823 1824-9.1829 10.1828- 5.1835	Incomplete
		BL,KCL	1.1828-9.1828 10.1828-5.1835	
Tralee Mercury	Tralee 1793-1839	NLI	2.1829-12.'36 1.1837-7.1839	
		BL,KCL	2.1829-12.1836 2.1827-7.1839	
Tralee Chronicle (Tralee Chronicle and Killarney Echo from 1857)	Tralee 1783-1881	NLI	3.1841-5.1881	Incomplete.
		BL, KCL	3.1843-5.1881	
Kerry Examiner and Munster General Observer	Tralee 1849-1856	NLI	8.1840-3.1856	Incomplete
		BL,KCL	8.1840-3.1856	Incomplete.
Kerry Star	Tralee 1861-1863	NLI	5.1861-3.1863	
		BL, KCL	5.1861-3.1863	
Kerry Evening Star	Tralee 1902-1914	BL,KCL	9.1902-3.1914	
		OCM	1902	vol. 11 (Indexes)
Kerry Independent	Tralee 1880-1884	NLI	10.1880-1.'84	Incomplete.
		BL,KCL	10.1880-1.'84	Incomplete.
Kerry News	Tralee 1894-1931	NLI	8.1927-6.1941	
		BL, KCL	1.1894-8.1920 8.1927-12.'29 2.1930-10.'30 1.1931-6.1941	
Kerry Weekly Reporter and Commercial Advertiser (Kerry Reporter from 1927)	Tralee 1883-1936	NLI	2.1883-8.1920 8.1927-12.'35	
		BL,KCL	2.1883-8.1920 8.1927-2.1936	
Kerry Advocate	Tralee 1914-1916	BL,KCL	7.1914-5.1916	
Kerry People	Tralee 1902-1922	BL,KCL	1902-1922	
Kerry Champion	Tralee 1928 - 1933	BL,KCL	8.1928-1933	

Newspaper Publication	Publishing D etails	Where Held	Time Frame	Notes
The Kerryman	Tralee 1904-4.1987	BL,KCL	1904-4.1987	
Killarney Echo and South Kerry Chronicle	Killarney 1899-1917	BL,KCL	1899-1917	
Kerry Sentinel	Tralee 1881 - 1913	BL,KCL	1881-1913	
Weekly Chronicle	Tralee 1873	BL,KCL	2.1873-6.1873	
Tralee Liberator	Tralee 1914-1939	BL,KCL	7.1914-9.1939	
Raymond's Kerry Herald	Tralee 1856	BL,KCL	1-1856-2.1856	
Munster Life	Tralee 1897	BL,KCL	3.1897-6.1897	
Kerry Press	Tralee 1916	BL,KCL	1916	

Extracts in Newspapers of Other Counties

Many newspapers published in Co. Clare, Co. Cork and Co. Limerick also contain useful information for the Kerry family history researcher. A number of these newspapers have indexes to biographical notices (usually births, marriages, deaths). These are listed in the following table:

Newspaper	Source	Period	Notes
Limerick Chronicle	OCM	1822 - 1840	Indexed in vol. 11
Limerick Gazette	OCM	1822-1840	Indexed in vol. 11
Ennis Chronicle	OCM	1827	Indexed in vol. 11
Limerick Evening Post	OCM	1828-1831	Indexed in vol. 11
Limerick Star and Evening Post	OCM	1835	Indexed in vol. 11
Limerick Standard	OCM	1838-1840	Indexed in vol. 11
Limerick Reporter	OCM	1839	Indexed in vol. 11
Munster Journal	OCM	1749-1850	Indexed in vol. 11

Newspaper	Source	Period	Notes
Cork Journal, Cork Chronicle, Hibernian Chronicle, Cork Gazette, Cork Evening Post, Cork Advertiser, Cork Mercantile Chronicle, Southern Reporter, Cork Morning Intelligence, Consititution, Volunteer Journal	Pub.	1754-1827	Indexed by Ms. Rosemary ffolliott. Original card index is in the library of the University College, Cork. Microfiche copies at GO, library of UCD and the New York Public Library.
Most Limerick, Ennis, Waterford and Clonmel Newspapers.	Pub.	1758-1821	Compiled by Ms Rosemary ffolliott.

The last two items may be purchased from the compiler, Ms. Rosemary ffolliott, c/o Glebe House, Fethard, Co. Tipperary. Two lesser known collections of newspaper extracts are Co. Kerry and Cork Births, Marriages and Deaths and Miscellaneous Events extracted from Co. Limerick and other Newspapers 1781-1821 by Basil O'Connell K.M. printed in OCM vol. 8 and the Nash collection of Co. Kerry newspaper cuttings recorded on LDS Film 0477616.

Chapter 12   National and Local Government Records

County Kerry has been administered by a number of different forms of government at both county and national level. The general upkeep of the county was controlled by Grand Juries until the 20th century. During the 18th and the 19th centuries the general populace gradually acquired the right to vote and the Grand Jury system declined. Another form of administrative organisation in Co. Kerry was the Poor Law Union Boards of Management which worked during the 19th century in the area of poor relief. At a national level persons from Co. Kerry were elected to the Irish parliament from 1613 to 1800. This chapter lists surviving records pertaining to all of these categories.

Grand Juries

Grand Juries, run by prominent community figures, administered the county. Several mid-eighteenth century statutes gave them powers to levy money for construction of roads, and later gaols and so forth. Each year the funds collected were divided amongst the baronies; a process known as presentment. The Grand Jury also ran the Assizes (local court sessions), conducted twice yearly. The following table lists sources pertaining to the grand juries of Co. Kerry. Most of the records are either transcripts or manuscripts from the records of the Co. Kerry Clerk of the Crown and Peace. Many of the sources are merely lists of members of the Grand Jury. The addresses of these persons are occasionally given.

Years	Description	Source
1893-1898	Grand Jury Presentment Books, The books cover Spring 1893 - Summer 1894, Spring 1895 - Summer 1896 and Spring 1897 to Summer 1898.	NAI

Years	Description	Source
1886-1899	Grand Jury Presentment Papers, The papers held are for Summer 1886,1893,1894-1898 and Spring 1890, 1893-1899.	NAI
1867	County Kerry Summer Assizes of treason-felony (Fenian) trials, part of an 8 volume set published in 1871 by Alexander Thom, Dublin.	KCL
1831	Petty Jury.	KEP 14/6/1876.
1825	Petty Jury, Spring Assizes.	KEP 2/5/1877.
1823	Petty Jury, May 17th.	KEP 25/4/1877.
1822	Petty Jury.	KEP 6/9/1876.
1821	Petty Jury, Summer Assizes.	KEP 14/6/1876.
1820	Petty Jury Panel.	KEP 24/9/1873.
1809	Grand Jury List, January 23rd.	KEP 5/5/1875.
1803	List of Co. Kerry Magistrates.	KEP 3/2/1897.
1801/2	Spring Assizes.	KEP 22/5/1872.
1798	List of Magistrates in Co. Kerry.	KEP 8/10/1873.
1785	Names and addresses of resident J.P's in Co. Kerry.	MAH vol 2.
1782	Jury List, Spring Assizes.	KEP 8/4/1876.
1781	Jury List, Summer Assizes.	KEP 8/4/1876.
1755	Grand Jury List, Spring Assizes.	MAH vol. 1.
1747	Grand Jury List, Spring Assizes.	MAH vol. 1.
1737	Grand Jury List.	KEP 22/4/1874.
1736	Resident J.P's for Co. Kerry. No addresses given	MAH vol. 2.
1714	Co. Kerry Magistrates attending a Tralee meeting.	MAH vol. 2.
1711	Grand Jury List, Summer Assizes.	KEP 31/10/1874 and 4/11/1874.
1679	Grand Jury List, Spring Assizes.	MAH vol. 1.
1585-1872	High Sheriffs of Co. Kerry. No addresses given.	MAH vol. 1.
1592 to 1697	An addendum for High Sheriffs lists 1585 - 1872.	MAH vol. 2.

National Government

"Parliamentary Representatives of Co. Kerry 1613-1800" are given in Appendix IV, *History of the Kingdom of Kerry* by M. Cusack, London 1871. The persons mentioned are usually the gentry/nobility. This list was reprinted in the KEP on February 1, 1888. After 1800 the Irish parliament was merged with the English parliament.

Poor Law Union Boards of Management

To alleviate the severe distress of the poor in Ireland and Britain, the Poor Law Act of 1838 provided funds to construct and run workhouses in which the poor were housed and fed in return for (often meaningless) work. The economic plight of the Irish was such that many workhouses were started. By 1848, for instance, there were six workhouses around the town of Tarbert in North Kerry giving aid to hundreds of people. The County Kerry Library holds the manuscript records of the Poor Law Union Boards' of Guardians. The records do not contain lists of those persons accomodated in the workhouse scheme, however your ancestor may be mentioned if, for some reason, they came to the notice of the Board or were actually an employee or administrator of the Board.

Poor Law Union	Manuscript	Period
Caherciveen	Minute Books	1905-1922
Dingle	Minute Books	1849-1920
	Rough Minute Books	1849-1921
Glin	Minute Books	1870-1891
Kenmare	Minute Books	1848-1921
	Financial Minute Books	1909-1914
Sneem Dispensary Comm.	Minute Books	1852-1895
	Quarterly Minute Books	1900
	Letter Books	1848-1864
Killarney	Minute Books	1840-1923
	Rough Minute Books	1840-1871
	Correspondence	1896-1921
	Local Govt. Correspondence	1895-1919
Listowel	Minute Books	1845-1922
	Rough Minute Books	1856-1899
Tralee	Minute Books	1840-1922
	Rough Minute Books	1845-1922
	Labourer's Act Minute Books	1887-1899
	Stat. Financial Minute Books	1904-1919
	Letter Books	1842-1903
	Correspondence	1908-1918
	Agreements	1889-1898

Electoral Records

Only a few documents listing eligible voters for the whole county exist. Electoral Registers for County Kerry 1906-1915, 1928-1939 are held at the NAI. The registers were deposited in the NAI from the Co. Kerry Clerk of the Crown and Peace. About 300 names and places of residence of voters in County Kerry in the 1918 Elections (districts of East, West, North and South Kerry) are given in *Kerry's Fighting Story 1916-1921*, The Kerryman (1947).

Further Reading

The following articles discuss further aspects of Local Government in Co. Kerry.

A Poll list for the Borough of Tralee, 1835 by Pádraig de Brún published in JKAHS no. 19 (1985).

List of Burgesses and Provosts of Tralee, 1776-1840 published in KEP June 20, 1888.

The Kerry 'Home-Rule' By-Election, 1872 by Brendan O'Cathaoir JKAHS, No. 3 (1970).

Local government in Dingle, Ardfert and Tralee in 1833 by Seán Ó Luing and published in JKAHS, No. 12 (1979).

Daniel O'Connell, Intimidation and the Kerry elections of 1835 by Gerard J. Lyne in JKAHS, No. 4 (1971).

Chapter 13   Military Records

Many different Militias and regiments were either based in, or conscripted from, Co. Kerry over the centuries. These military units were organized by local gentry (i.e. the militia and yeomen), by the Government, or the British army. Records are very diverse in nature, and well-scattered among different archives. The surviving records usually contain only officer's names, ranks and sometimes addresses.

Original Documents

The Public Record Office, Kew in London, UK has a collection of papers for the disbanded Kerry Militia Regiment. This collection, the most complete source of military papers extant for Co. Kerry, is stored in the collections of War Office Records at the PROK, and has beem microfilmed by the LDS.

War Office Volume	LDS Film	Description	Time Frame
v.410/1	0917573	General order book, letters, etc.	1858-1859
v.410/1	0917574	General order book, letters, etc.	1859-1873
v.410/2	0917574	Regimental letter book	1856-1857
v.410/3	0917574	Circulars of the Kerry Militia Inspector General	1871-1876
v.411/1-2	0917574	Court Martial Book	1793-1858
v.411/3	0917574	Bounty Board Book	1771-1814
v.412/1-3,5	0917575	Regimental letter book	1855-1876
v.412/4	0917575	Staff and Regimental order book	1867-1872

All able-bodied Protestant males between ages of 16 and 60 were, by law, part of a militia unit. A manuscript listing the conscripts in all militias in Co. Kerry in 1761 is held by the Genealogical Office in Dublin.

Transcripts

Transcripts of lists of men in various Co. Kerry militia and regiments are printed in the following:

Kerry Volunteer Regiments in 1779 and 1782 in the Kerry Archaeological Magazine, Vol. II (11) (1913) and Vol. V (21) (1919) respectively.

Munster Provincial Regiment of Foot, Officer Lists are printed in KEP 18/4/1874.

Munster Militia Commissions are printed in the KEP of 15/5/1874.

List of Kerry Militia of 1808 printed in the Kerry Archaeological Magazine, Vol. V (21) (1919).

Changes to Officer's ranks were often given in newspapers (see p. 63). For example, the Limerick Chronicle of February 26, 1806 lists appointments in the Kerry Militia, as does the Leinster Journal of August 1, 1795. The Leinster Journal of November 12, 1795 contains a list of appointments to the Irish Yeomanry Corps, some of whom were stationed in Co. Kerry. These newspapers are available at the NLI.

Chapter 14 Education Records

In early times education in Co. Kerry was provided by monasteries, seminaries and by private teachers. By the 17th century many schools were in operation. Petty, writing in the 1670s, and Story, in 1691, both mention a strong element of classical education throughout the county. The Penal Laws of the 18th and early-19th centuries required that Catholics were only permitted to be educated within the county and were barred from attending Trinity College, Dublin. Hedge schools evolved in many parishes to provide Catholic education. Although "Catholic" education was technically proscribed, in practice it is clear that many Catholic-run schools existed in the late 18th century. However, few records survive. After the institution of the national school system in the early 19th century, access to schools rapidly improved although records are still sparse.

School records

Any surviving lists of students for Co. Kerry schools prior to 1900 are retained locally. There is no set policy on access. The best approach is to determine if a school existed in the parish for the period you are searching and then write to the parish priest. Lewis's "Topographical Dictionary" (see p. 18) often mentions the existence and location of schools in the civil parish and town descriptions. A series of articles entitled "Kildare Place Society in Kerry: Schools and Lending Libraries" by Pádraig de Brún (JKAHS *12* (1979), p. 63; *13* (1980), p. 83) provides a useful list and map of many schools in Co. Kerry for the 1810 to 1840 period. The Kildare Place Society was a charitable organisation that assisted schools by donating books, Bibles and other school materials. Students' names are not listed in these articles. Occasionally the names of correspondents to the KPS, usually parents or local leaders, are given. The teachers of the schools are listed and indexed in a glossary.

The article titled *Some documents concerning Valentia Erasmus Smith School 1776-1795* by Pádraig de Brún JKAHS, no. 15/16 (1982/1983) lists students at the school during this period. The articles *Castleisland Charter School* (JKAHS *1* (1968)) and *Primary education in Kerry one hundred years ago* (JKAHS 5 (1972)) by Michael Quane also provide details of schools in Co. Kerry.

The NAI holds some National school records such as applications for school commencement (1832-1889), registers made by inspectors (from 1835) and salary books (from 1834). Class sizes are recorded but no roll-calls of students exist in this collection. The names of teachers are generally listed. The records are listed in an index in the public search room at the NAI.

University Education

Trinity College Dublin, founded in the year 1593 by Royal charter, has published details from its student registers up to the year 1860 in *Alumni Dublinenses* by Burtchaell G.D. and Sadlier, T.N., Volume 8 of OCM contains extracts from this work; year of study, student name, age, name(s) of parent(s) of Co. Cork and Co. Kerry students for 1593 to 1860. An example of the information in the OCM extracts is as follows:

1682 Chas., son of Bryan Connor, a. 19
1701 Mce., a.19, son of Bernard Connor
1706 Thoms, 18 son of Thomas, cleric
1711 Watkin, a.18, son of Thomas
1718 Mce., 18, son of Rev Connor.

The offspring of wealthier Co. Kerry residents were also educated at schools and universities throughout Europe, details of which are often included in published family histories (see. p. 75).

Chapter 15   Family Histories

Up until the start of the twentieth century, the types of families in Kerry which had their family history documented in manuscripts and books were mainly Nobility and Gentry. With their position of control, combined with the Co. Kerry intrigue for family history, this group are well represented in surviving material. For many notable Irish clans (tuatha) quite detailed histories exist up to the mid 17th century. These pedigrees pass back towards the time of Christ, often in intricate detail. These genealogies have been passed on as oral tradition over more than a thousand years. They are partly myth and partly fact.

It is important to remember that a document or manuscript containing a family tree or history does not necessarily constitute proof of family relationships. The facts presented should be evaluated by the researcher. If the original primary sources are still available they should be re-checked. The situation and credentials of the person who created the document or manuscript should also be considered. Could they feasibly have had access to all the information required to produce the material? By all means check for a family history but realise that finding one may not be the end of the search, although it will usually be, at least, a good head-start.

Published Co. Kerry histories

The following table lists the published pedigrees that I have found in researching this book. Some of the families are documented in several sources, which are noted as (1), (2) and so forth in the Sources column of this table.

Surname	Place	Sources
Blennerhassett	Co. Kerry	(1) *MAH*, pp. 33 notes alliances with many other Co. Kerry familiesand covers period 1688-1736. (2) *Burke's Irish Family Records*, 1976.
Brewster	Co. Kerry	*Irish Ancestor*, vol. 3, no. 2, 1971.

Surname	Place	Sources
Burtchaell	Brandondalle	*Visitation in Ireland*, vol. 1, 1911.
Butcher	Killarney	*Visitation in Ireland*, vol. 2, 1911.
Collis-Sandes	Tieraclea	*Burke's Landed Gentry of Ireland*, 1884.
Crosbie	Ballyheigue	*Burke's Irish Family Records*, 1976.
Denny	Tralee	*Lodge's Peerage of Ireland*, p.298.
Duggan	Nohavaldaly	*OCM*, vol. 6.
FitzMaurice	Co. Kerry	(1) *JKAHS*, no. 3, (1970) by K.W. Nicholls. (2) *Lodge's Peerage of Ireland*, vol. 2.
Fuller	Glashmacree	(1) *Visitation in Ireland*, vol. 4, 1911. (2) BCG , p. 655.
Gun	Rattoo	(1) *OCM*, vol. 7. (2) *Burke's Landed Gentry of Ireland*, 1912.
Herbert	Currens	*Burke's Landed Gentry of Ireland*, 1904.
Hickie	Kilelton, Aghavallen civil parish.	(1) *Hickie of Kilelton* by T. Pierce in The Shannonside Annual, Tralee, 1957. (2) *Burke's Irish Family Records*, 1976.
Hurly	formerly of Bridge House	*Visitation in Ireland*, vol. 6, 1911.
Leslie	Tarbert	(1) *Irish Builder*, 1890. (2) *The Leslies of Tarbert, Co. Kerry and their forebears*, P. Pielou, Dublin, 1935.
Lucy	Co. Kerry, Co. Cork	*OCM*, vol. 6.
McCarthy Mor		*The Book of Munster by Rev. E O'Keefe*, 1703 reprinted in *OCM*, vol. 11.
McGillicuddy	The Reeks	*The McGillicuddy Papers*, by W. Maziere-Brady, Longmans, Green and Co., London, 1867.
McSwiney	Co. Kerry	*JKAHS*, no. 13 (1980) by Gerard J. Lyne.
Mahoney	Knockavone, Brosna parish	*Irish Ancestor*, vol. 13, no. 1, 1981.
Markham	Nunstown and Callinaferry	*Irish Ancestor*, vol. 16, no. 2, 1984 by Brian de Breffney.

Surname	Place	Sources
Millington-Synge	Co. Kerry, Co. Cork, Shropshire U.K.	*OCM*, vol. 6.
O'Connor-Kerry	Carrigafoyle, Aghavallen	(1) *BCG* p. 381. (2) *Irish Pedigrees*, J.O'Hart, pp. 330. (3) *The Shannonside Annual*, vol. 1, no.1, Tralee 1956.(4) *O'Connor Clan History*, ed. by Pat Harrold, Cork, 1987. (5) *Notice on some branches of the O'Connor Kerry family*, compiler unidentified,early 19th century, Ms 667, NLI. (6) *Kerry clans andconfiscations*, by the Rev C.J. O'Connor-Kerry, n.3624, p.3242, NLI.
O'Connell	Lakeview and Ballybegan	(1) *Visitation in Ireland*, vol. 2, 1911. (2) *Burke's Irish Family Records*, 1976. (3) *Notice on some branches of the O'Connor Kerry family*, compiler unidentified, early 19th century, Ms 667, NLI, also discusses the O'Connell family of Kerry.
O'Keefe	Co. Kerry, Co. Cork	*OCM*, vol. 6.
Orpen-Palmer	Killowen	*Visitation in Ireland*, vol. 3, 1911.
Pierce	Co. Kerry, Co. Cork.	*OCM*, vol. 6.
Sandes	Aghavallen, Kilnaughtin, Murher parishes	(1) *Visitation in Ireland*, vol. 4, 1911. (2) *Burke's Landed Gentry of Ireland*, 1884.
Taylor	Dunkerron	*JKAHS*, no. 17 (1984), p. 61, is an article on an unpublished history of this family written in Canada in 1912.
Thompson	Tralee	*Burke's Landed Gentry of Ireland*, 1912.

Published Collections of Family Histories

There are a number of general collections of published family histories that may be consulted for family history research. The Burke family have produced a number of different collections; *The General Armory of England, Scotland,*

A Handbook of
County Kerry Family History,
Biography, &c.,

BY

The Rev. H. L. L. DENNY, M.A., F.S.G.,

Author of 'Anglo-Irish Genealogy,' 'Memorials of an Ancient House,'
'The Manor of Hawkesbury,' Etc., Etc.

(Ancient Seal of the Borough of Tralee).

Compiled for the Archæological Group

OF

The County Kerry Society.

MCMXXIII.

WRIGHT & HOGGARD, PRINTERS, BRISTOL.

Ireland and Wales, London, (1884, 1912) and *Irish Family Records, (1976)*. Other sources include *R.F. Cronnelly, Irish Family History*, Dublin, (1865); J. Foster, *The Royal Lineage of our noble and gentle families. Together with their paternal ancestry*, 2 vols, London, Hatchards (1887); de Ruvigny, Nobilities of Europe, (1910); J. O'Hart, *Irish Landed Gentry*, Dublin, (1899); J. O'Hart, *Irish and Anglo-Irish Gentry*, Dublin, (1884); and J. Windele, *Genealogies of North Cork and East Kerry*, Dublin, (1865).

The Denny Handbook of Sources

The Reverend Sir Henry L.L. Denny compiled *A Handbook of County Kerry Family History and Biography in 1923*, the year after the Public Record Office fire. Denny surveys the damage caused by the fire to Co. Kerry family history sources. Reverend Denny takes stock of what remains, particularly in local collections and lists their sources. Some of the sources given include manuscripts in his own collection and in the possession of people living as far from Co. Kerry as Jerusalem. The families mentioned in this volume are:

Allanson-Winn , Alton, Amory,

Babington, Bateman, Benner, Benson, Bland, Blennerhasset, Bolton, Bradshaw, Brennan, Brewster, Browne, Buckley, Busteed, Butcher, Butler,

Cameron, Cantillon, Carew, Carrick, Cashell, Chute, Collins, Collis, Collis-Sandes, Colomb, Conway, Copinger, Cranfield, Cronin, Cronin-Coltsmann, Crosbie, Crumpe,

Damer, Day, De Moleyns, Denny, Dowdall, Dowling, Downing, Drew, Eager, Elliot, Ellis,

Fagan, Fairfield, Ferriter, Fitzgerald, Fitzhenry, Fitzmaurice, Fosbery, Fuller,

Gentleman, Ginnis, Godfrey, Gorham, Graves, Griffin, Groome, Gun, Hare, Harman, Harnett, Harte, Heard, Herbert, Hewson, Hickson, Hilliard, Hoare, Huggard, Hurly, Hussey, Hyde,

Jeffcott,

Langdon, Lauder, Lawlor, Leader, Leahy, Leake, Leeson-Marshall, Leslie, Leviston, Leyne, Lyne,

MacCarthy, McClure, McElligott, MacGillicuddy, McLoughlin, MacSwiney, Madgett, Magee, Magill, Mahony, Markham, Marshall, Martelli, Mason, Maynard, Meredith, Moore, Morgell, Moriarty, Morphy, Morris, Mulchinock, Mullins, Murphy,

Nagle, Nash, Neligan,

O'Connell, O'Connor, O'Donoghue, O'Donovan, O'Falvey, O'Halloran, O'Mahony, O'Reilly, Orpen, O'Shee, O'Sullivan,

Paine, Palmer, Paradine, Parr, Pellican, Petty, Plummer, Ponsonby, Prenderville, Purdon,

Quill,

Race, Raymond, Rice, Roche, Roome, Rowan, Ryeves,

Sandes, Saunders, Scanlan, Sealy, Segerson, Shewell, Shiercliffe, Skiddy, Spotswood, Spring, Spring-Rice, Stack, Stokes, Stoughton, Strange, Sugrue, Supple,

Talbot, Talbot-Crosbie, Thompson, Townsend, Trant, Travers, Trench, Twiss, Vauclier, Vesey-Fitzgerald,

Walker, Weekes, Willoe, Wilson, Wren,

Yielding.

Chapter 16   General Kerry References

This chapter lists further general reference works, local histories, guides and bibliographies relevant to Co. Kerry ancestry research. Printed material such as books, pamphlets and journal articles may provide the family history researcher with knowledge of local history of the part of Co. Kerry in which their ancestor resided. Many of these works are available at the KCL, the NLI and major libraries in Australia, England and the United States.

The most complete bibliography of Co. Kerry is Margaret Stack's *A Bibliography of Co. Kerry*. Specialist works of Irish bibliography include Baumgarter, and Eager. These works should be consulted if the reference sought is not listed in this chapter (see below).

Published Works

Allman, J. *Causeway, location, lore and legend*, Naas, 1983.

Barrington, T.J. *Discovering Kerry*, Dublin 1976.

Barrow, J. *A Tour round Ireland: through the sea coast counties in the autumn of 1835*, London, 1836.

Baumgarter, R. *Bibliography of Irish Linguistics and Literature*, Dublin, 1986.

Bourke, F.S. *A Handlist of books on Killarney*, Bibliog. Soc. Ir., vol. 6, no. 2 1953.

Casey, A. E. O'Kief, *Coshe Mang, Slieve Lougher and Upper Blackwater in Ireland*, 15 volumes plus collated source volume, Birmingham (USA), 1952-1971. One of the most valuable references for ancestry searching.

Coleman, J.C. The mountains of Killarney, Dundalk, 1948.

Coleman, James, *Bibliographia Kerriensis: A list of topographical works relating to the county of Kerry*. Kerry Arch Mag, No.1, 1908, p38-44.

Cronnelly, R.F. *Irish Family History*, Dublin 1865.

Cusack, M.F. *History of the Kingdom of Kerry*, London 1871.

Denny, Rev H.L.L., *A Handbook of County Kerry Family History, Biography &c,*. compiled for the Archaeological Group of The County Kerry Society, 1923.

Donovan, T.M. *A Popular History of East Kerry*, Dublin 1931.

Eager. A.R. *A Guide to Irish Bibliographic Material*, Library Assoc., London 1980.

Feehan, Sean, *The scenery and character of Kerry*, Cork 1975.

Finuge Heritage Society *A Span Across Time: Finuge. A Folk History by the Finuge Heritage Society and ANCO*, 1986. Local history and description.

FitzErin, Rev John F., Day *Killarney Sketches*, 1862.

Gaughan, J. Anthony, *Listowel and its vicinity*, Mercier Press, Cork, 1974.

Harty, Rev. J., *The Cistercian Chronicles*, 1640 reprinted in OCM vol. 6.

Hayward, R., *In the Kingdom of Kerry*, Dundalk 1950 and again by Dundalgan Press in 1976.

Hickson, M., *Selections of Old Kerry Records, Historical and Genealogical*, 2 vols, Watson & Hazell, London, 1872-1874.

Hickson, M., *Place- and Surnames in Kerry. Royal Soc. of Antiquaries*, Ireland Journal, vol. xxi and xxiv.

Hogan, Rev. E., *Description of Ireland, 1598*, Dublin, 1878. The part relating to Munster province reprinted in OCM vol. 15.

Holly, D. & J., *Tarbert on the Shannon*, Donegal Democrat, Ballyshannon, Donegal, May 1981. Local history and description.

Keane, L., *Knocknagoshel: Then and Now,*.Kerry County Library, 1985.

Kavanagh, J., *Historical Guide to Ardfert*, published prior to 1986.

Kennelly, P., *The History of the O'Rahilly's Ballylongford G.A.A. Club*, C.N.B. Press, Cork, 1986. Past and recent local history.

King, J.S., *County Kerry Past and Present: Handbook to Local and Family History*, Hodges, Figgis and Co., Dublin 1931. The A to Z encyclopedia of all things about Co. Kerry. Reprinted by Mercier Press, Cork, 1984.

King, J.S., *History of Kerry*, vols 1 to 6. Printed serially in The Kerry People, 1909, 1910, 1912-1914.

Lavelle, D., *Skellig: Island outpost of Europe* Dublin, 1976.

Leslie, J.B., *Ardfert and Aghadoe clergy and parishes*, Dublin 1940.

Lewis, F., *Muckross Folk Museum, Killarney*. Killarney, 1975.

Liber Hiberniae Establishments of Ireland, Volume 1 is reprinted in OCM vol. 6, Volume 2 in OCM vol. 7.

McCarthy, S.T., *Three Kerry Families: (Mahoney, Conway, Spotwood)*, 1923.

MacKay, J., *In Iveragh and the Dunkerrons in The Ten Islands and Ireland*, 1919.

McMoran, R., *Tralee: a short history and guide to Tralee and environs*, 1980.

Mould, D.C. Pochin, *Valentia: portrait of an island*, Dublin, 1978.

Mulcahy, M., *Summer Sands of Youth: Memories of Ballinskelligs*, Killarney Advertiser, Killarney, 1981. Local descriptions.

O'Ciobhain, B., *Barony of Dunkerron North, Co. Kerry*, Dublin, 1978.

O'Connell, B., *Bibliography of Co. Kerry, 1599-1917*, From the Kerry Evening Post of 1870-1917 in OCM vol. 15.

O'Conchuir, D., *Corca Dhuibhne, its People and their Buildings*, Ballyferriter, 1977. Local history and descriptions.

Concubhair, P. & Mac Gearailt, T., *North Kerry Football Board: The Clubs of North Kerry 1924-1984*, Fitzsimons Printers, Shanagolden, Co. Kerry, 1981. Local history, with names, dates and photographs.

O'Connor, B., *Description of Kerry*, 1751.

O'Connor, M., *Kerry Pastoral, 1719*, re-printed in Early English Poetry, Ballads of Popular Literature of the Middle Ages, Percy Society, vol. vii, 1842.

O'Connor, P., *North Co. Kerry: Territorial Organisation and Settlement before c.1600 AD*, unpublished PhD thesis, University College, Dublin, 1979. History.

O'Donovan, J., *Antiquities of the County of Kerry*. Royal Carbery Books, Cork 1983. Local and ancient history and description.

O'Hanlon J., *Index to materials relating to the history and topography of County Kerry in the Ordnance Survey Office*, Kilkenny S.E. Ir. Arch. Soc. Journal, 1864 to 1866, pp. 486-490. Historical records lists.

O'Shea, Fr. K., *Castleisland: Church & People*, Geography, Local history.

Stagles, J.& R., *The Blasket Islands, Next Parish America*. In Island Series 4, O'Brien Press, Dublin, 1977. Geography and local history.

O'Sullivan, Thomas F., *Romantic hidden Kerry: a description of Corkaguiny*, Tralee, 1931. Geography.

O'Sullivan, William, *Williams Molyneux's geographical collections for Kerry* in JKAHS, no. 4 (1971), pp. 28-47.

Ryle, Maurice P., *Kingdom of Kerry*, 2nd edn, 1903. History.

Smith, C., *The Ancient and Present State of the County of Kerry*, Dublin, 1756 and reprinted in OCM vol. 10.

Stack, M.A. *A bibliography of Co. Kerry*. Thesis for Fellowship of the Library Assoc.of Ireland, 1968.

Stoakley, T.E. Sneem, *The Knot in the Ring*, Leinster Leader, Naas, Kildare, 1986. Local history.

Synge, J.M., *In Wicklow West Kerry and Connemara*, Dublin, 1911. Reprinted 1919 and 1980. Local history

The Kerryman, *Kerry's Fighting Story of 1916*, The Kerryman, Tralee, [n.d.]. Excellent reference about the men and women who fought in the Troubles in County Kerry. Gives descriptions of local units, and East Kerry reprinted in OCM vol. 7.

Windele, J., *Genealogies of North Cork and East Kerry*, reprinted in OCM vol. 7.

Local History: A bibliography. Printed by the Kerry County Library in 1956.

Index to Manuscript and Periodical Sources

Richard J.Hayes, *Manuscript Sources for the History of Irish Civilisation* was first published in 1965. A three volume supplement was published in 1979. The initial 11 volumes is an index of Irish manuscripts found throughout Ireland and in many private libraries and collections. The volumes are indexed separately by Name of Persons, Subject, Places (within each county) and Date. Also available is Richard Hayes' *Periodical sources for the history of Irish Civilization* which, like the above is well indexed and occasionally up-dated.

This large collection of information requires some imaginative searching to make the best use of the resource. The recommended approach is to look under the name of the civil parish or nearest town or village, and also under the name of the family you are searching for. It is also a useful index to the manuscript holdings of the NLI itself up to 1965; and to 1979.

REFERENCES ADDED IN 2nd EDITION

Kelly, Liam; Lucid, Geraldine and O'Sullivan, Maria, *Blennerville, Gateway to Tralee's Past*, Tralee 1989;

Lysaght, Paddy, The River Feale, Limerick 1987.

Moriarty, Joseph, *Ballyheigue Beside the Sea*, 3rd edition, History, Legend and Lore.

O'Connor, Tommy, *Ardfert In Time Past*, Ardfert, 1990.

Stafford, T., *Pacata Hibernia*, Dublin 1810.

Tarrant, B. and O'Connell, G., *Exploring the Rich Heritage of the North Kerry Landscape*, Listowel, 1990.

Chapter 17   Useful Addresses

Irish Addresses

Finuge Heritage Society,
Teach Siamsa, Finuge House,
Co. Kerry:

The Society has a research service and is collecting records for the Lixnaw and Listowel areas.

Genealogical Office (GO),
42 Kildare St, Dublin 2:

Includes the State Heraldic Museum and the Office of the Chief Herald. The records, which include family papers, wills and pedigrees, are not generally accessible to the Public in the GO Library. The GO also offer a research service. Many of the major sources are also available on microfilm at the NLI.

Irish Land Commission (ILC),
Keeper of Records, Records
Branch, Land Commission,
Dept. of Agriculture, Kildare
St, Dublin 2:

Holds land ownership from the 1880's to the present day, plus documents from earlier estate dissolutions.

Irish Land Registry,
Keeper of Records,
Chancery St., Dublin 7:

Contains the records of land whose ownership has been registered. Not all property is included since some land ownership is established by Deeds rather than registration. Provides the Folio number to a property documented at the ILC.

*Kerry Archaeological and
Historical Society,*
c/o Hon Secretary, County
Library, Moyderwell, Tralee,
Co. Kerry:

The Society publishes an annual Journal, of much use to the Co. Kerry ancestry researcher. Field trips and lectures are also organised by the Society.

Kerry Heritage & *Genealogical Centre,* Bishop's House, Killarney, Co. Kerry:	Official indexing centre for Kerry but will not be offering a service until all indexing is completed in 1995.
Muckross House, Killarney, Co. Kerry:	Includes a folk museum and much material relating to the Killarney area. Operates a research service.
National Library of Ireland, Kildare St, Dublin 2, Ireland:	Holdings include microfilms of most Catholic parish registers, Griffith's Valuations, Newspapers, Estates and Family Papers, Commercial and Social Directories and Maps.
National Archives, Bishop Street, Dublin 8:	Holdings include Griffith's Valuation Manuscripts, Tithe Applotment Survey Returns, some Church of Ireland Parish records, census material for 1901 and 1911, Estate Records, Wills and Administrations and the Records of the Co. Kerry Clerk of the Crown and Peace.
Registry of Deeds, Henrietta Street, Dublin 1:	Holds records of legally registered Deeds since 1708.
Registrar-General's Office, 8-11 Lombard St, Dublin 2:	All civil records of births, marriages and deaths from 1864 and Church of Ireland marriages from April 1845. Indexes may be consulted in the public search room for a fee.
Trinity College Library, Trinity College, Dublin 2:	Holds a large collection of Manuscripts and printed books and also records of the college estates, some of which were in Kerry.
Royal Irish Academy, 19 Dawson St, Dublin 2:	Holds a large collection of valuable manuscripts and printed books.

Representative Church Body, Library, Braemor Park, Rathgar, Dublin 14:	Holds some Church of Ireland registers for Co. Kerry.
State Paper Office, Dublin Castle, Dublin 2:	Includes records of tranported convicts, the State documents on the 1798 and successive rebellions, and other papers related to the English administration of Ireland.
Valuation Office, 6 Ely Place, Dublin 1:	Holds copies of maps showing location of properties listed in Griffith's, and subsequent Valuations.

Australian Addresses

National Library of Australia, Parkes Place, Canberra, ACT 2600:	Holds copies of OCM, JKAHS and JSK.
Genealogical Society of Victoria, Floor 6, 252 Swanston St, Melbourne, Vic 3000:	Holds part of OCM (Vols. 1,5) plus records related to Irish Australian immigrants, and IGI.
Society of Australian Genealogists, Richmond Villa, 120 Kent St, Sydney, NSW 2000:	Holdings include OCM, and Commercial and Social Directories.
State Library of New South Wales, Macquarie St, Sydney, NSW 2000:	Holdings include OCM, and Commercial and Social Directories.
State Library of Queensland, William St, Brisbane, QLD 4000:	Holdings include OCM, and Commercial and Social Directories.
State Library of South Australia, North Tce, Adelaide, SA 5000:	Holdings include OCM, and Commercial and Social Directories.

State Library of Victoria,   Holds many Co. Kerry books plus Griffiths
304-328 Swanston St,   Valuations printed returns, Commercial and
Melbourne, Vic 3000:   Social Directories, Journals, Index to Irish
                                Convicts (1788-1886).

State Library of Western   Microfiche of Ordnance Survey Maps.
Australia,
Alexander Library Building,
James St, Perth, WA 6000:

The Irish Link,   Publishes the Journal of Irish Australian
P.O. Box 135, South   Family History. Has copies of the Index to
Melbourne, Vic 3205:   Townland Maps (Ordnance Survey 1913)
                                and the journal often lists available family
                                histories of Australians descended from Co.
                                Kerry folk. A copy is sent to the KCL.

United States Addresses

Samford University Special   The library owns the Albert E. Casey
Collections Library,   collection from which the OCM series was
Samford University,   published. Also holds copies of the Tithe
800 Lakeshore Drive,   Applotment books for Co. Kerry. A public
Birmingham, Alabama,   search room and a Consultancy Service are
35229, USA: available.

Genealogical Library,   Centered in Utah with branches throughout
Church of Jesus Christ of   the world, the Church has major collections
Latter Day Saints,   of microfilmed Irish records — marked as
Salt Lake City,   LDS throughout this guide. Also publishes
Utah, USA: the IGI database.

United Kingdom Addresses

British Library Newspaper   One of the major collections of Co. Kerry
Collection,   newspapers. Much of the relevant material
Colindale Annex, London: has been microfilmed and is available at the
                                KCL.

British Museum (Printed Books/Manuscripts), Greater Russell Street, London:

Holds many relevant books and manuscripts about Co. Kerry including OCM, MAH and JSK.

Public Record Office, Ruskin Avenue, Kew, Richmond, Surrey, TW9 4DU:

The records of the Disbanded Regiments (see p. 00) for the Co. Kerry militia are kept here.

Index

A

Abbeydorney 32, 33
Abbreviations 8
Administrations 45
Administrative Divisions 11
Aghadoe 15, 16, 29, 32, 34, 52, 82
Aghanagran 22
Aghavallen 16, 22, 29, 34, 35, 52, 53, 59,
   61, 76, 77
Aglish 16, 29, 31, 33, 35, 53
All Ireland Heritage 25
Allanson-Winn 79
Alton 79
Amory 79
Analecta Hibernica 26
Annagh 16, 29, 35
Annascaul 29, 30
Archer, Rev. F. 39
Ardcrone 53
Ardfert 15, 16, 29, 30, 31, 33, 35, 47, 53,
   70, 82
Ardfert Abbey 53
Assizes 67

B

Babington 79
Ballinacourty 16, 25, 30, 35
Ballincuslane 16, 29, 30, 35
Ballinskelligs 82
Ballinvoher 16, 25, 29, 30, 31, 33, 35
Ballybunion 30, 32
Ballyconry 16, 30, 31, 32, 35
Ballyduff 16, 25, 30, 32, 33, 35
Balyferriter 24, 30, 31, 33
Ballyheigue 16, 30, 35, 76
Ballylongford 29, 44
Ballyloughran 60
Ballymacdonnell 26

Ballymacelligott 16, 29, 30, 33, 35, 53
Ballynacourty — *see* Ballinacourty
Ballynaglish 16, 30, 35
Ballyseedy 16, 30, 35
Baptismal records 28
Barony 11, 17, 18
   Clanmaurice 17, 45, 59
   Corkaguiny 17, 59
   Dunkerron 17, 58
   Dunkerron North 17,82
   Dunkerron South 17
   Glenarought 15, 17
   Iraghticonnor 17, 45, 59, 61
   Iveragh 17
   Maguinihy 17, 24
   Trughanacmy 17, 24, 59
Barraduff 52
Barron, John 20
Bateman 59, 79
Beaufort, Rev. D. 39
Benner 79
Benson 79
Betham Abstracts 46
Blacker-Douglas 61
Bland 79
Blennerhasset(t) 60, 75
Blennerville 37
Boherbue 33
Bolton 79
Bonane 31
Books of Survey and Distribution 25
Bradshaw 79
Brandonvale 76
Brennan 79
Brewster 75
British Library 25, 63, 88
British Museum (Printed
   Books/Manuscripts) 26, 89